CASE STUDIES IN
ARCHAEOLOGY SERIES

SERIES EDITOR
JEFFREY QUILTER
RIPON COLLEGE

THE CEREN SITE

**A Prehistoric Village Buried by
Volcanic Ash in Central America**

Figure 1–1. Map of Mexico and northern Central America. Prehistorically, Mesoamerica included central and southern Mexico and all of Central America through El Salvador and western Honduras.

THE CEREN SITE

A Prehistoric Village Buried by Volcanic Ash in Central America

Payson Sheets

University of Colorado, Boulder

Harcourt Brace Jovanovich College Publishers

Fort Worth   Philadelphia   San Diego   New York   Orlando   Austin   San Antonio
Toronto   Montreal   London   Sydney   Tokyo

Editor in Chief	Ted Buchholz
Acquisitions Editor	Christopher P. Klein
Project Editor	Angela Williams
Production Manager	J. Montgomery Shaw
Senior Book Designer	Serena Barnett Manning
Composition	Norman Haskell

Address for Editorial Correspondence
Harcourt Brace Jovanovich, Inc., 301 Commerce Street, Suite 3700, Fort Worth, TX 76102

Address for Orders
Harcourt Brace Jovanovich, Inc., 6277 Sea Harbor Drive, Orlando, FL 32887
1-800-782-4479, or 1-800-433-0001 (in Florida)

ISBN: 0–03–078856–0

Library of Congress Catalogue Number: 92–70636

Printed in the United States of America

2 3 4 5 6 7 8 9 0 1 067 9 8 7 6 5 4 3 2 1

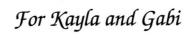

For Kayla and Gabi

Foreword

ABOUT THE SERIES

These case studies in archaeology are designed to bring students, in beginning and intermediate courses in archaeology, anthropology, history, and related disciplines, insights into the theory, practice, and results of archaeological research, whether in the field, laboratory, or library. The authors are also teachers, and in writing their books they have kept the students who will read them foremost in their minds. These books are intended to present a wide range of archaeological topics as case studies in a form and manner that will be more accessible than writings found in articles of books intended for professional audiences, yet at the same time preserve and present the significance of archaeological investigations for all.

ABOUT THE AUTHOR

Payson Sheets was born on New Year's Day in 1944 in Colorado, a fourth generation Coloradan. He did his undergraduate studies at the University of Colorado in Boulder. As an undergraduate he had a number of different majors, including chemistry, math, art history, and geology. He was unable to decide on a major because so many were of interest and he dropped out of school for a year to think it over. He spent most of that year traveling around Europe, and became fascinated with archaeological sites and the reasoning process necessary to reconstruct past societies from their material remains left in the archaeological record. That solidified his decision, and he has been an archaeologist ever since.

Sheets completed his graduate studies at the University of Pennsylvania by receiving his Ph.D. in 1974. During his graduate studies he spent two seasons in fieldwork at Chalchuapa, El Salvador, where he met Fran Mandel, who had come from California to join the project. They married three years later and now have two children, Kayla and Gabrielle.

Sheets has conducted archaeological research in the southwestern United States, in western Canada, and in Guatemala, El Salvador, Nicaragua, Costa Rica, and Panama. He taught at Pitzer College (Claremont, California), California State University at Fresno, and since 1974 at the University of Colorado, Boulder, where he has chaired the department.

Sheets has published numerous books and articles, including (with Don Grayson) *Volcanic Activity and Human Ecology, Archeology and Volcanism in Central America: The Zapotitan Valley of El Salvador,* and (with Fred Lange and Suzanne Abel-Vidor) *The Archaeology of Pacific Nicaragua.*

ABOUT THIS CASE STUDY

It is a great pleasure for me and a significant event for archaeology that Payson Sheets' *The Ceren Site* should serve as the first book published in the new case studies series. While other sites in the Western Hemisphere might vie for the title of the "American Pompeii," the exceptional quality of the Ceren site lies in the fact that it is in a region where there is usually little hope of finding much preserved at archaeological sites beyond those artifacts made of durable materials such as stone and fired clay. The richness of the archaeological record available at Ceren is truly astounding and provides professionals, students, and laymen alike with a new view of the Maya past. Many aspects of Maya life that formerly could only be approached through inference or supposition have now been laid bare for study.

No student of archaeology passes through his or her beginning classes without some exposure to the fascinating peoples of southern Mesoamerica, and interest in the Maya has recently increased, with new developments occurring as much in quiet libraries as in field studies. Within my 20 years as a student of archaeology, the Maya have passed from prehistory into history as the process of decipherment of their hieroglyphs has reached a point where the succession of royal dynasties, wars, and other changing political fortunes of the Maya elite can now be discussed in detail. But, while the movement into history is a great scholastic achievement, the daily lives of rural farmers fall outside of hieroglyphic texts. Although archaeology generates much of its popular appeal through the spectacular discoveries and discussions of the pomp and circumstance of great civilizations, it also prides itself in its attention to the daily lives of those outside the circles of power. Thus, Professor Sheets's discoveries at Ceren as discussed in this book take on added importance in providing us with a detailed view of the dwellings, utility buildings, artifacts, and gardens of a small group of farmers, as a counterpoint to the rich and fascinating views we are obtaining of the ruling classes of Maya society. Exciting artifacts and excellent preservation by themselves do not make good archaeology, however. It also takes skill and imagination to retrieve information with accuracy and efficiency. Professor Sheets is to be commended for his abilities in excavating Ceren with precision, and I am sure readers will be fascinated as well as informed as to how he successfully excavated the site.

The focus of this book on the detailed examination of the organization of Maya households and the way they were investigated will give students and teachers much to discuss regarding the problems and potentials of investigating the past through archaeology. In addition, Professor Sheets offers a rich bonus in his discussion of conducting archaeology in El Salvador in the midst of its civil war. No archaeology student, nor for that matter professional, should contemplate research without taking into account the significance of an archaeological project on local political, social, and economic realities, and this is as true for work in North America and Europe as it is for the Third World. For archaeologists and local people alike, present day concerns can, and sometimes should, outweigh more lofty academic goals. I hope that all our contributors to this series will be as forthcoming as Professor Sheets in providing their readers with discussions of the contexts in which their archaeological work took place.

The Ceren Site offers a wealth of information and ideas to discuss and ponder. The author and I hope that students and teachers will both enjoy and learn from this book.

JEFFREY QUILTER
Series Editor
Ripon, Wisconsin

Preface

A principal objective of this monograph is to share what we have learned about life in Central America during the Classic Period, some 1400 years ago. In particular, we will be looking at households at the Ceren site in what is now El Salvador. During the past two centuries, archaeologists have learned a lot about the elite, the wealthy, and the powerful, by excavating their palaces, tomb burials, and associated areas. The traditional bias of archaeology was to excavate the visually spectacular artifacts, architecture, and art, and that bias still exists. The elite lived in palaces and other substantial buildings that tend to preserve better than housing of other segments of the society. Certainly we should not think that the elite were unimportant, as they were the decision makers at the top of society. Further, there have been exciting developments in translating the hieroglyphs that describe major events in their lives, including birth, marriage, assuming the leadership position, battles, and death. However, the balance of knowledge is vastly in their favor. Far too little is known about the "silent people of prehistory," the commoners who did the basic, everyday work to support the elite. We know little about their daily lives, their houses, their artifacts, their activity areas, and other details. Our knowledge of the Maya is "top-heavy," and we need to know more about the vast majority of the population, the commoners.

The main impediment to understanding the commoners is that their houses, activity areas, and artifacts tend to preserve very poorly. Much of that is due to the heat and humidity in tropical climates that facilitate rapid decomposition of organic materials. Adobe (earthen) architecture lasts in a tropical climate only as long as the thatch roof remains in good condition, but thatch roofs need to be replaced every few years. When the roof is gone in an abandoned structure, the rains rapidly erode the walls and floors, and the sun dries and cracks the architecture. Also, families abandoning their houses take their most valuable possessions, leaving behind only things that they consider not worth carrying with them. The heat, humidity, termites, and bacteria of the tropical environment facilitate rapid decomposition of organic materials. Thus, archaeologists trying to excavate and understand the average remains of prehistoric housing that was abandoned for hundreds of years have two strikes against them before they begin. They must deal with a greatly impoverished data base.

Ceren is a striking exception to the above generalization. It was a village on the southern periphery of the Maya area that was suddenly buried by a volcanic eruption. Had it not been for that eruption, Ceren after its abandonment probably would have been just like many village archaeo-logical sites: barely worth excavating. However, that did not occur, as the eruption preserved the village in an exceptional fashion. That eruption was not preceeded by warnings such as earthquakes, and it came from the sudden opening of a volcanic vent under a nearby river, not from a mountain that was recognizable as a volcano before the eruption. In addition, it apparently happened at night, after the evening meal but before people went to sleep. People did not have time to take their possessions with them, as they would have in an orderly abandonment. Rather, we have been excavating their possessions from their buildings as they were "frozen in time" by the sudden arrival and deep burial of volcanic ash from what is now known as Laguna Caldera volcano.

Although decades of excavations remain for the future, we have learned much about family life at Ceren from the various seasons of excavations conducted so far. Previously we had no indications of the sophistication in adobe domestic architecture. Now we know that the Ceren residents routinely constructed multiple structures for various uses within each household. It appears that each household had a domicile building for sleeping, eating, and various daytime activities, and a storehouse, a kitchen, and sometimes other buildings. The Ceren residents roofed and protected the structures with very ample thatch roofs, most of which cover more area outside the walls than inside. The areas under the eaves and outside the walls were used for storage, as covered walkways, and for various activities such as grinding corn.

Households had gardens either immediately adjoining buildings, or separated from them only by a narrow walkway. With only one exception, all plants were cultivated in rows that line up with the dominant architectural orientation of the site, 30 degrees east of north. The exception is the agave (maguey) cactus garden of Household 4, where plants are haphazardly placed. Because agave plants sprout themselves from the roots of older plants, it would be difficult to maintain order among them. The agave leaves were used for fiber to make rope and twine. Other than the agave, all plants line up quite precisely with the architecture in the very ordered landscape. Garden plants include corn (maize), cacao (chocolate), and a range of other plants that have yet to be firmly identified.

Three maizefields have been found farther from structures, and most corn plants are mature, indicating that the eruption occurred at the end of the growing season. Many maize plants were doubled over, with the ears of maize still attached to the stalk, a storage-in-the-field procedure that still is performed in traditional areas of Mexico and Central America. Some maize ears were husked in the field, and others maintain the husks as they remained on the doubled-over stalk. One area has juvenile maize, only one to two feet tall, which probably is a second planting during the middle of the rainy season. These plants and the stage of growth of other annual plants indicate that the eruption which buried Ceren occurred during August.

Once food had been harvested and brought in from the field, it was stored in the household in a variety of facilities. Some grains were stored in large, fired clay vessels with tight lids, and other vessels were suspended from ceiling beams by ropes. In both cases, ants and mice occasionally got inside and were eating grains. Corn was stored in Structure 4 in a large corn crib made of poles and clay. Some grains were stored up in roofing, and some were suspended, such as chiles hanging in bunches.

Three special purpose buildings apparently served more than one household. Structure 3, the biggest building excavated from the site so far, seems to have been a community center, where political and social functions may have occurred. The massive but low Structure 9 has an elegant adobe dome and a large firebox inside, and it probably was a sauna utilized by a few families. Structure 12, surfaced white, with numerous scattered artifacts, might have been where a shaman ("seer") practiced, although other interpretations are possible.

The Ceren site provides us with an unusually clear window into the prehistoric past with which to view family activities on the frontier of the Maya area. It is an extraordinarily well-preserved site, because of the sudden arrival of copious amounts of volcanic ash. That volcanic ash did not allow people to selectively remove artifacts, and it largely stopped natural processes of decomposition. What we see at the site is surprisingly sophisticated and ample domestic architecture. Public architecture was varied and generally of very solid construction. The artifacts within households are striking for their abundance and, in many cases, for their elegance and beauty.

ACKNOWLEDGEMENTS

The first people I wish to acknowledge are the Salvadoran workers who labored with us under the intense sun and high humidity of the Zapotitan Valley day after day. They deserve much credit for the great increase in our knowledge of family life in the valley as it was practiced some 14 centuries ago. They are Victor Manuel Murcia (foreman and longtime friend), Salvador Quintanilla, Salvador Ramirez Rojas, Marco Tulio Chinchilla, Jose Humberto Portillo, Pedro Ismael Giron, Jose Antonio Menjivar, Antonio Rivera Espinoza, Jose Mario Quintanilla, Lazaro Amaya Lopez, Hector Armando Guevara, Jaime Arturo Moron, Jose Cesar Cordova, Elias de Jesus Rivera, Francisco Alberto Escamilla, Carlos Nelson Leiva, Rodrigo Bautista Canton, Osmin Elisandro Granados, Pedro Ramirez Galdamez, Reyes Nelson Alvares, Rodrigo Hernandez Leon, Jose Guadalupe Funes Canton, Rene Antonio Quintanilla Carabantes, Salvador Antonio Quintanilla, Rene Antonio Coca de Paz, and Juan Rivera Rodas.

The project scientific staff worked long and hard, under less than ideal circumstances. I want to express my appreciation to Marilyn Beaudry-Corbett, Dan Miller, Hartmut Spetzler, Dan Wolfman, Andrea Gerstle, Brian McKee, Harriet Beaubien, Fran Mandel Sheets, David Tucker, and Jeannie Mobley-Tanaka.

Many people in the Ministry of Education facilitated our research. An immense debt of gratitude I owe to Lic. Zulma Ricord de Mendoza, Director of the Patrimonio Nacional. Arq. Maria Isaura Arauz de Rodriguez, Director of the Patrimonio Cultural, has been of assistance throughout the project. The assistance of Evelyn Sanchez and Gloria de Gutierrez is appreciated. The staff in Restoration and other sections of the museum have helped many times, in so many ways.

Manuel Arrieta of IBM loaned us a computer and printer in two consecutive years, which assisted in data analysis and writing of the preliminary report. Our friend Peter got us access to the Bayer Pharmeceutical's airplane, from which we obtained good aerial photographs of the site and the nearby volcanos. Coronel Ochoa of CEL graciously loaned us his helicopter to take additional airphotos of volcanos and sites. We appreciate the fact that the owners of surface-to-air missiles did not dispatch one in our direction while we were taking the airphotos. Peter Doty was his usual enthusiastic and helpful self. Ricardo Recinos continued to be the best friend an archaeological site could have. ABANSA assisted by donating money that was used to expand the number of Salvadoran workers. TACA assisted the project with free airline tickets to bring certain specialists into the country. Bob Dance, Pamela Corey-Archer, and the USIS staff helped the project in manifold ways. David and Beverly Kitson, AID, were instrumental in setting up donations by many people in the U. S. community in El Salvador. The Hotel Presidente, particularly Alicia de Landaverde, was gracious and beneficent to us on a number of occasions.

The Patronato Pro-Patrimonio Cultural has been instrumental in the success of the research. This non-profit organization has backed the project in many ways. I particularly wish to thank Mario Cristiani, Ana Vilma de Choussy, Juan Carlos Choussy, Neto Raubusch, and Ricardo Recinos.

Principal funding for the research was awarded by the U. S. National Science Foundation, most recently by grant #9006482. Their financial support is heartily appreciated. The University of Colorado made a large contribution by awarding me a Faculty Fellowship so that I could be in El Salvador from August 1990 through January 1991 and April 1991 conducting the research.

Jeffrey Quilter and Brian McKee critiqued an earlier version of this manuscript. They cannot be held responsible for any of its shortcomings, but they certainly deserve recognition for improvements in its readability, order, and logic.

Contents

1
Introduction

This monograph focuses on a prehistoric village in tropical Central America (Figure 1–1) that was buried suddenly by volcanic ash about 1400 years ago. People did not have time to abandon the village in an organized way and take their important possessions with them. Thus, the site provides an unusual opportunity to explore family and village life in great detail. The site was discovered recently and has had a total of only ten months of research conducted within it, to date. It consists of a series of three households along with some specialized buildings. Because the site was buried by five meters (17 feet) of volcanic ash, specialized instruments are necessary to discover individual structures. The eruption was not a single blast but a complex series of explosions that has required the trained eye of a geologist to understand. The sudden burial by moist and fine-grained volcanic ash has resulted in unprecedented preservation of organic materials, particularly in a tropical climate. Biologists have identified the seeds, the wood, the thatch roofing, and animal remains.

Although this is a monograph in archaeology, it shares certain objectives with monographs in ethnography to present a different culture to undergraduate students in a readable and informative manner. Ethnographers have a huge advantage over archaeologists in that they can talk to the people they are studying. Unfortunately, as archaeologists, our informants died many centuries ago. We cannot hear what they say, we cannot question them and check their answers, we cannot record their language. However, we are immersed in their material culture. Our strength is in the results of their behavior. And, in contrast to most ethnographers, we can study them for large periods of time. The emphasis of this monograph is in the material culture of the Ceren site and how people in the site related to their natural and social environments. Given the nature of the sudden burial of Ceren by volcanic ash, our emphasis is on the community functioning just before the eruption instead of over time.

Ethnographic research typically is done by a single investigator moving into the society to be studied and living there as inobtrusively as possible. In contrast, archaeology more commonly is a team effort, and the

Figure 1–2. The flat valley floor of the Zapotitan Valley, El Salvador, with volcanoes in the background. Santa Ana Volcanic complex is at the right, with Izalco Volcano in the center. The crew members are doing an archaeological survey in the periphery of the San Andres site; the middle worker is standing on a housemound, all that is left of a gradually abandoned house the same age as the Ceren houses.

Ceren project is an example. The research team is composed of students, specialists, and local workers. The students, primarily from the University of Colorado, are selected for their relevant coursework, their abilities in Spanish, and their abilities to live under difficult conditions and contribute to the overall research effort. Certain specialists have been essential to the success of the research, particularly in geophysics, volcanology, and biology. Their contributions are described in Chapter 3.

THE NATURAL ENVIRONMENT

The Ceren site, named after the nearby town of Joya de Ceren ("Jewel of Ceren"), is located at an elevation of 450 meters (1500 feet) alongside the Rio Sucio, in the Zapotitan Valley (Figure 1–2) of what now is El Salvador. The climate and natural vegetation is tropical, with hot daytime temperatures year-round. Fortunately, the area cools off rather well at night. The average annual temperature is 24 degrees Celsius (75 degrees Fahrenheit), with a low in December of 22 degrees (67 degrees F) and a high in April of 26 degrees (83 degrees F). The daytime–nighttime fluctuation is greater than this annual seasonal fluctuation. In the United States, the real difference between winter and summer is temperature. However, in Central America the real difference between their "invierno" (winter) and "verano" (summer) is precipitation. The rainy season is the invierno and the dry season is the verano.

The site area receives an average or mean of 1700 millimeters of precipitation, but the standard deviation is 300 millimeters. This means that in one third of the years the area receives more than 2000 or less than 1400 millimeters of rainfall. Occasional years receive more than 2300 or less than 1100 millimeters.[1] The mean is a statistical abstraction, and almost never does that precise amount of rain fall in a particular year. The rainfall variability is what is significant, and a farmer must be able to cope with years of low rainfall as well as years of abundance. He[2] must also cope with years of overabundance of rain, as that can cause erosion and thus result in production declines for years in the future. I had that pointed out to me, as a fresh and rather naive graduate student in El Salvador, while talking with a peasant farmer. I commented to him that an average of 1700 millimeters was ideal for corn (maize) agriculture. He said that, yes, it would be ideal, but when did the average ever show up? Rather, he has to deal with the lean years as well as the soggy years to feed his family every year. Obviously, his family could not tolerate a single year with minimal food production, and so he maintained various strategies to deal with uncertainty. He viewed the environment as opportunity and as hazard, and he accommodated to both simultaneously.

The rainfall in the Zapotitan Valley, as with most of the Pacific slope of Central America and Mexico, is highly seasonal. The dry season extends from November through April and the rainy season from May through October. The dichotomy is strong, with only 6 percent of the rain falling in the dry season, and almost all of that in the "transitional" months of November and April. The rains usually begin in May, but that can be early or late May, or occasionally in late April or even in early June. All these factors can cause great agricultural difficulties, as maize seeds, for instance, need to be planted just before the rains, so that they can germinate in a warm, porous soil, but then they need rain in significant amounts to begin their rapid growth. Because most of the Salvadoran countryside cannot be irrigated, annual crops can grow only during the rainy season.

The successful traditional agriculturalist (Figure 1–3) must also adapt to the form in which the precipitation comes. Most storms are gentle and allow the moisture to filter into the soil. However, the strong cloudbursts that often occur during July through September can severely erode exposed soil. Traditional agriculturalists in many areas of Central America plant maize along the tops of ridges that block the lateral movement of water, minimizing erosion and aiding infiltration. To our surprise, we found the technology of blocking ridges fully developed at Ceren 1400 years ago.

Another factor to be coped with is wind. While the Zapotitan Valley is not unusually windy, strong winds do accompany cloudbursts during the rainy season. That is particularly dangerous for maize, as it is unusually vulnerable to wind-throw. Planting on the ridges, with some soil packed up around the maize stalks, is of assistance. In the valley today traditional agri-

Figure 1–3. Two traditional agriculturalists planting a field at Chalchuapa, El Salvador, which is essentially unchanged from the prehistoric past. The field was cleared of vegetation during the dry season, and low ridges were built up. The planting is done in May, at the beginning of the rainy season, by making a hole along the top of the ridge with the digging stick, putting four or five maize kernels in the hole, and filling in the hole by kicking dirt into it. Each agriculturalist wears a gourd with seed in it strapped to his waist.

culturalists plant in May so the harvest can be completed by September. That has the benefit of not exposing the growing maize plants to the "nortes," the strong winds from the north that are the southernmost tail of big North American winter storms. Those generally strike in November, December, or January, when the fields are clear of crops.

The strong seasonality of precipitation means that many small and medium-sized streams only flow during the rainy season. Because people need sources of fresh water year-round, it is not surprising that prehistoric settlements in the valley tended to cluster along permanent streams, near springs, and around the large lake in the center of the valley.

Biologically, El Salvador lies within the Neotropical Realm, extending from southern Mexico through lowland South America. This area is characterized by high biomass and diversity in plants and high diversity in animals but not high biomass. Unfortunately, the population explosion in the country during the past 150 years has almost destroyed all natural habitats. But it should be noted that this recent habitat destruction is not the first, as expanding human populations toward the end of the Formative Period, by about the time of Christ, had fundamentally altered most areas under 1000 meters (3000 feet). Then, the Ilopango eruption, evidently in AD 175, wiped out the remaining vegetation along with animals, insects, and other critters. The tropical environment was able to recover from catastrophe within about three centuries, as evidenced by people moving into the valley and establishing the Ceren village. Human pressure on the natural environment increased to another prehistoric maximum toward the end of the Classic Period, about AD 900. Population declined somewhat during the Postclassic period, from AD 900 to 1500, and declined precipitously in the 1500s and 1600s as diseases introduced by the Spanish devastated native populations. New World Indians had no resistance to diseases such as yellow fever, malaria, influenza, and measles, and the population of the country dwindled to only a few tens of thousands (Barron Castro 1942).

Daugherty (1969) has reconstructed the native climax vegetation of the Zapotitan Valley. Most of the area was covered by a dense deciduous forest, watered by the rains of the wet season. Many of the trees shed their leaves during the dry season to preserve moisture. The most common trees are balsam (*Myroxylon balsamum*), madre cacao (*Gliricidia sepium*), ceiba (*Ceiba pentandra*), conacaste (*Enterolobium cyclocarpum*), amate (*Ficus* spp.), volador (*Terminalia obovata*), ramon (ujushte or ojushte; formal name *Brosimum terrabanum* or *alacastrum*), and cedar (*Cedrela* spp.). Also growing in the forest, particularly where encouraged or planted by people, were avocado, jocote, nance, papaya, sapote, and anona. All these have edible fruits. Along water courses a lush evergreen forest grew that did not need to shed its leaves in the dry season. At higher elevations, between 1000 and 2000 meters (3000 to 6000 feet), a pine and oak forest predominated. Only one species of pine was there, but there were a dozen species of oak. Above this was the cloud forest, generally enshrouded by mist, with trees covered with orchids, vines, and other plants.

Unfortunately, the Salvadoran fauna has been even more devastated than the flora as of late. Only mice, rats, cockroaches, flies, mosquitoes, ants, and vultures have done well. The mammals, reptiles, amphibians, birds, and fish have suffered. Of these, birds have suffered least, with some 480 species and subspecies still in the country. A bizarre result of the civil war that has plagued the country since 1979 is that vegetation and animals have been recovering in "conflictive zones" where people fear to tread. Trees have recolonized many of these depopulated areas, and deer and other animals have come back into areas where they had not been seen for many generations.

As with most of Central America, the Zapotitan Valley is a volcanic landscape. The valley is dominated by the huge volcanic complexes of San Salvador Volcano on the east and Santa Ana Volcano on the west. Some volcanos are quite recent, such as Izalco. It started erupting from a side vent of Santa Ana in 1770 and continued for two centuries. It was so visible from the Pacific Ocean, day and night, that sailors called it the "lighthouse of the Pacific." It built itself from nothing to a cone 1900 meters high, but then it ceased erupting in 1965. That was particularly unfortunate, as a fancy hotel and volcanic observatory had just been constructed on nearby Cerro Verde, and the official opening ceremonies were to be held a couple of months later.[3]

TABLE 1. EXPLOSIVE ERUPTIONS DEPOSITING AIRFALL VOLCANIC ASH IN THE ZAPOTITAN VALLEY

Eruption:	Date:	Sq. Km. Buried:	Plume Direction:
Playon	AD 1658	30	SSW
Boqueron (V.San Sal)	est. AD 1000	300 >7cm	SSW
Laguna Caldera	est. AD 600	20	Southerly
Ilopango	AD 175–76	10,000 >50cm	NW
Coatepeque	40,000–10,000 BC	?	?

Notes on Table 1: The Boqueron eruption, from San Salvador Volcano, is not yet radiometrically dated, and could be a couple of centuries before or after this date. The Laguna Caldera eruption is dated by a series of radiocarbon analyses, with a composite date of AD 590, plus or minus 90. Ilopango's composite radiocarbon date is AD 260, plus or minus 114, but the recent finding of ash matching Ilopango in an ice layer dated to AD 175–176 in Greenland probably is the best dating. Coatepeque has not been radiometrically dated, but is estimated. It formed the base materials for much soil development in the Zapotitan Valley before the more recent eruptions. It was a big eruption, perhaps on the scale of Ilopango. The other eruptions were much smaller and had more localized effects. From Sheets (1983:5–6).

The frequency of lava flows over the past few hundred years also gives some indication of how volcanically active the area is. Within the valley, San Marcelino erupted in 1722 and buried about 15 square kilometers under lava. El Playon erupted in 1658 and buried a similarly sized area under lava, and most recently, San Salvador Volcano covered about 30 square kilometers with lava in 1917. Accompanying that eruption was a violent earthquake that destroyed San Salvador and other nearby communities. The crater lake inside San Salvador Volcano boiled away just before the earthquake and the lava eruption.

In addition to Santa Ana and San Salvador, other volcanic cones and mountains encircle the big, broad valley. The bottom of the valley is a wide plain that held Lake Zapotitan in the center. The soils in the flat valley bottom, weathered from volcanic ash, were particularly fertile. Freshly fallen volcanic ash is not fertile, as it is basically fine-grained rock. However, after weathering releases nutrients, it can be very fertile, and so there is some truth to Juan Valdez's claims of fertility in volcanic soils, as depicted in coffee advertisements on television.

Table 1 lists five explosive eruptions that deposited airfall volcanic ash in the Zapotitan Valley (Figure 1–4). Only two of the eruptions were massive regional natural disasters, Coatepeque and Ilopango. It is not known if people lived in the area when Coatepeque erupted. However, it is important in that there was sufficient time after its eruption for a very mature soil to form, and that soil was very fertile. It had high organic content, had a balanced pH very near seven, and was high in trace elements that facilitated plant growth. Such soils, with their high clay content, were the source of adobe material for construction at the Ceren site and for clays that were worked into vessels and other ceramic artifacts. There must have been a number of explosive eruptions affecting the valley between Coatepeque and Ilopango, but we have yet to find any direct evidence of them.

The Ilopango eruption was massive, depositing a meter to a few meters of white, acid volcanic ash in the valley, evidently in the year AD 175. This killed most vegetation within the valley, polluted water supplies, and rendered most fields uncultivatable. The Zapotitan Valley was largely abandoned by people for two or three centuries, while the volcanic ash weathered into soil, and plants and other animals gradually recolonized the area. Beaudry (1983) notes the lack of Early Classic Period (AD 300–600) ceramics in the Zapotitan Valley during the valleywide survey, and this probably is evidence of the long time of abandonment.

Ceren may be one of the earlier sites colonized as people moved back into the Zapotitan Valley. Their pottery is a Middle-to-Late Classic assemblage, based on Beaudry's analysis (1983). The radiocarbon dates support this, placing the occupation at around AD 590, plus or minus 90. However, they were to live there for perhaps only about a century, to be interred rapidly by the eruption of Laguna Caldera Volcano. It is located only 1.4 kilometers to the north, about a mile away. According to the studies of volcanologists (Hoblitt 1983, Miller 1989), Laguna Caldera erupted suddenly with a series of base surge and pyroclastic flow deposits (fast moving clouds of ash and gasses) and airfall layers. It was not a volcano prior to the eruption but was only a place where an underground fissure opened up and magma moved upward. It formed a volcanic cone during the eruption and has not erupted since. Although it was devastating to the Ceren site and probably other nearby sites, it was not a regional natural disaster like Ilopango. Rather, it adversely affected only about 20 square kilometers. The Laguna Caldera eruption is described in more detail in the volcanology section.

A few centuries after the Laguna Caldera eruption, San Salvador Volcano erupted. The volcanic ash came from the main crater, called the large mouth, or "Boqueron." The Boqueron eruption has never been dated by radiocarbon or other quantitative means, but an estimated date is circa AD 1000, plus or minus a century or two. It deposited a thick layer of pasty wet volcanic ash over the southeast corner of the Zapotitan Valley, but the Ceren area received only a thin layer, perhaps 20 or 30 centimeters thick. The area was reoccupied, at least lightly, after the Boqueron eruption, as evidenced by some artifacts being found stratigraphically above it.

The most recent explosive eruption to affect the Ceren area was the eruption of El Playon Volcano, located about four kilometers east. It began erupting in AD 1658 and continued into 1659. It deposited a layer, almost a meter thick, of coarse, dark ash. In the more than three centuries that have passed since its eruption, soils have yet to fully recover; they are thin and

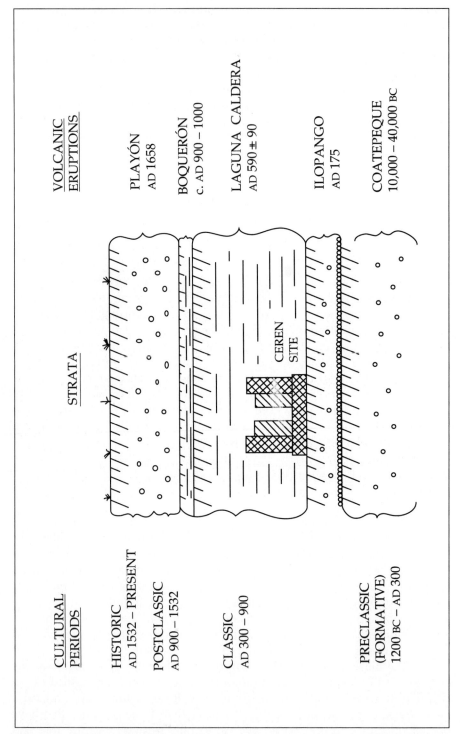

Figure 1–4. Schematic diagram of stratigraphy in the Zapotitan Valley, with the earliest eruptions at the bottom, up to the most recent eruption in 1658.

moisture is not well-retained for plant growth. Much like they did in the past, people in the area today are taking advantage of the benefits of living in a volcanically active area, but they also suffer difficulties.

Earthquakes are common in the Zapotitan Valley. In fact, it is an unusual month to not feel one. Every few years, or at least ever few decades, an earthquake occurs that does structural damage and causes some injuries and deaths. We will see in subsequent chapters how the prehistoric residents of Ceren developed an architecture that was very earthquake resistant and superior to much construction in Central America today.

THE SOCIAL ENVIRONMENT

The Zapotitan Valley is a small part of the large Precolumbian culture area known as Mesoamerica. Mesoamerica extended from central Mexico into northern Central America, and was the area in which complex societies developed. A number of civilizations emerged in this area, of which the Olmec, the Maya, and the Aztec probably were the best known. All civilizations based their agriculture on maize and beans, and all areas had sedentary villages as far back as 2000 BC. Cultures developed stratified social systems, with the elite making decisions for the commoners, composed of farmers and other workers. The religions became more formalized and hierarchical and were directly associated with the state. The economies became more centralized, with the elite controlling long distance trade and redistribution of many commodities within the society. The physical manifestations of this centralization in the social, economic, and religious systems are not difficult to see in the archaeological record. Within the capital of each civilization the religious center is marked by tall pyramids surrounded by broad plazas where the multitudes would gather to participate in religious events and be impressed by the supernatural powers of their religious leaders. A central marketplace, usually not far from the religious center, would be maintained for exchanges of food, clothing, tools, spices, pigments, and other goods. The palaces, where the elite lived, often overlooked the plazas and marketplaces where they could keep track of the elaborate systems under their control.

Mesoamerican archaeologists have traditionally emphasized the elite. It is not surprising that most Mesoamerican archaeologists have preferred to excavate a palace rather than the humble dwelling of a farmer, or to excavate a pyramid rather than the plain religious shrine in the periphery of town. The massive construction of the palaces and main pyramids make them much easier to find, and the preservation is generally much better than is the preservation of the humble dwellings of the commoners. Also, as archaeology was still under the "fancier is better" approach, it was assumed without question that it was better to search for the elegant grave offerings of fancy jade masks and gold ornaments (Indiana Jones syndrome) than to look for the things that were important and available to most of the population. Thus, we now know much about the very top 10 percent of society in

Figure 1–5. One of the pyramids of the San Andres site, the political-economic-religious hub of the Zapotitan Valley during the Classic Period. The pyramid was partially excavated and consolidated. The stairway probably led to a temple on top, made of poles with a thatch roof. The plaza is at the left. Beyond the pyramid, in the sugar cane field, are unexcavated residences of elite and commoners. The Ceren site is only five kilometers away.

Mesoamerica, but we know very little about the remaining 90 percent. Only recently have archaeologists turned directly toward learning about the silent people of prehistory. This book is dedicated to their finding a voice and becoming known for the first time.

The Zapotitan Valley had completely recovered demographically from the Ilopango eruption by the Late Classic Period (AD 600–900). Black (1983:75) found a total of 42 sites in his survey of the valley. They were composed of 14 hamlets, 14 small villages, 7 large villages, 3 isolated ritual precincts, 4 large villages with ritual construction, 2 secondary regional centers, and 1 primary regional center. Because a probability-based statistical sample of 15 percent of the valley was surveyed, the estimates for the valley as a whole would be a total of 280 sites, and most of the above site types can be multiplied by 6.67 to obtain the estimated valleywide figure. There was only one primary regional center, however, which was the site of San Andres (Figure 1–5) in the center of the valley. It was the religious, political, and economic center of the valley, and it is certain that people from Ceren would go there for special purposes. San Andres and Ceren are only five kilometers apart in a straight line.

Those special purposes probably included major religious events. Routine religious practices were handled in the household or the community, but the priests at San Andres would be involved with the principal ceremonies. It evidently was the economic hub of the valley, importing obsidian from the Ixtepeque source in Guatemala, and providing occupational specialists to shape the cores and use percussion and pressure techniques to make sharp knives, scrapers, and utility cutting tools. It is likely that San Andres also mediated the trade of jade into the valley. Jade occurs farther into Guatemala than the obsidian, and it is probable that the same traders brought both. Jade was used for beads and axes in the Ceren site. Also standardized are hematite red paint cylinders, probably purchased at market, perhaps in San Andres. The source of the very pure cinnabar (mercuric sulfide, HgS) is unknown, but it is likely that it was under centralized authority as well. Finally, it is probable that San Andres served as the political center of the valley population. If disputes arose that could not be resolved locally, people probably went to San Andres for final adjudication. Disputes could have emerged over access to arable land or other resources, over possessions, or a variety of other issues.

Black (1983:82) estimates that there were between 40,000 and 100,000 people living in the Zapotitan Valley during the Late Classic Period, from about AD 600 to 900. Based on his figures, populations nucleated somewhat during the Early Postclassic (AD 900–1200), and declined only slightly. They further declined during the Late Postclassic (AD 1200–1500) to barely more than half of the Late Classic figures. It is clear from the hierarchical and interrelated nature of the social, political, economic, and religious system in the valley during the Late Classic that Ceren was functioning within a complex culture. There was no such thing as a "typical" site of the time, as each was performing different functions within the whole society. The range in size of sites was great, and some have pyramid complexes, while others do not. The reality is in the diversity and interrelatedness of social components.

SITE DISCOVERY AND HISTORY OF RESEARCH

The Ceren site was first discovered by a bulldozer operator in 1976. He was leveling a low hill just north of what we now call the Ceren site, to create a flat platform on which to build some grain storage silos. As he was working, he noticed that the blade cut the corner of a building buried by volcanic ash. He hopped down and dug around a bit, finding more of the floor and edge of the building and some pottery that was inside the building. Acting more responsibly than most bulldozer operators in any country, he called the National Museum in San Salvador and notified them of his discovery. It took the museum three days to send someone to the site to look it over and assess its potential importance. The museum archaeologist thought it was very recent, and thus not very important, and gave the green light to keep bulldozing. A number of structures were completely destroyed and their contents decimated. One other building had its northern part bulldozed away, but the rest was left in the cut bank. The bulldozing was damaging, but the site would still be unknown to us had it not been done. It is unfortunate that its significance was not recognized upon first discovery.

Two years later I was in El Salvador with a team of students from the University of Colorado doing an archaeological survey of the Zapotitan Valley. I had not learned of the discovery from people at the museum but heard of it from people living near the site when I was asking for permission to inspect their property. Hearing that it probably was a historic or possibly recent house buried under volcanic ash, I had no expectations that it could be prehistoric. However, I was puzzled that I did not know about such a recent eruption, since I understood the volcanic eruptions of the area rather well; so I set out to find the remains of the buried building. It was relatively easy to find, in the bulldozer cut at the south end of the silo property. A floor and the tops of a couple of adobe columns were immediately visible, as was a low platform a few meters to the west. I grabbed my trowel and began clearing volcanic ash off the hardened clay floor of the house, looking for artifacts that would help date the building (Figure 1–6). I expected to find a bit of plastic, part of a soda bottle, some aluminum foil, or perhaps some newspaper that would shed light on its date. The first artifacts I found were some pieces of Classic Period polychrome (multicolor painted) pottery that I could date to about AD 500–800, based on the style and manufacturing techniques. Even that did not shake my belief that the house was recent; the thatch roof was so well-preserved, collapsed to the floor under all the overburden of five meters (16 feet) of volcanic ash. The houses of most peasant agriculturalists in the area today have some prehistoric artifacts in them. Farmers often bring interesting pieces of pottery or other artifacts back to their houses; thus it is a rare farmer who does not have his own collection.

However, after a few hours of excavating I had found only prehistoric artifacts and not a single artifact that I could identify as historic or recent. I began to perceive two very different possibilities: (1) I was on the brink of a massive professional embarrassment if I prematurely announced the find of these structures as prehistoric, and they turned out to be recent, or (2) they were in fact prehistoric, and therefore the site is of extreme importance. The real key was dating, and I carefully collected samples of the thatch roofing for radiocarbon dating. My colleague Sam Valastro at the University of Texas Radiocarbon Laboratory would be able to date the samples by measuring their radioactivity. The older the sample, the less the radioactivity, and I could collect large samples to increase the accuracy. There is an advantage to submitting thatch roofing over pieces of wooden roofing support, or pieces of charcoal from a fire pit or hearth. Those pieces could be from inner growth rings from trees that had lived quite a while earlier than the burial of the house by the volcanic ash. Analyzing earlier growth rings would tend to push the date back in time. In contrast, thatch needs to be replaced about every four years, so there was little difference in the age of the organic material and the time I wished to date, the eruption and burial of the site. I eagerly awaited the telephone call from Sam, and when it came, he said that all samples were about 1400 years old. All samples dated since then have substantiated the 1400-year age as well, so there is no longer any doubt about the antiquity of the site.

Figure 1–6. The Ceren site after limited excavations in 1978; the bulldozer had removed the northern part of the domicile (left) and the workshop (right). The two adobe columns and the floor of the domicile can be seen, along with the doorway between them that leads to the innermost room. The white layer of volcanic ash below the building is from the Ilopango eruption; it buries the clay-rich soil that is the source of construction material.

We were able to excavate a little in two buildings, now called Structures 1 and 5, before the end of the field season in 1978. We returned in 1979 and 1980 to do geophysical work, searching for more structures buried under the volcanic ash, and we were successful. However, the civil unrest was worsening, and we did not get back to Ceren until 1989 to excavate more buildings. The 1989 and 1990–91 seasons were successful in excavating quite a few buildings that belonged to three households, as well as some specialized buildings (Figure 1–7). The emphasis of work at the site, at least for the next few years, will be on conservation. The architecture is so fragile that careful work must be done to every square inch to make sure that these delicate buildings have a long future. It would be irresponsible to take them from their "time capsule" and bring them abruptly into the present, without giving them the best conservation possible to ensure their future.

ABANDONMENT

When a family leaves their house for just a short time, they leave artifacts in their position of use or storage, and a relatively complete household assemblage is left intact. However, when a family decides to abandon a house, the most important and valued possessions are taken along, and others are sold or bartered. After the family departs, other people in the area generally take things that may be useful to them, including parts of the architecture. Burial of the Ceren village was sufficiently rapid that the site was not abandoned by its inhabitants, in contrast to most prehistoric villages. Dean (1987) documented the strong bias in material remains as modern households in northern Honduras are gradually abandoned and people remove many important items. Lange and Rydberg (1972) noted the same as a family abandoned their domicile in Costa Rica, leaving behind a greatly impoverished material culture. Wilshusen (1986) documented how the mode of abandonment affects preservation of artifacts and activity areas and the superior nature of sudden abandonment for detailed reconstruction of Anasazi behavior, in the United States' Southwest. A wide range of abandonment modes are being explored by archaeologists. By comparison, the Ceren site anchors an end of the spectrum; it never was abandoned, and we can learn so much about life there.

PRESERVATION

The sudden volcanic burial did not allow for a sudden abandonment, thus preserving artifacts in their position of use or storage. In addition, the nature of the volcanic ash preserved organic materials in a way almost unprecedented in a tropical wet environment. The finger swipes of food left in pottery serving bowls are still preserved; we found their dirty dishes! (Forks were not invented until recently, in the 1700s, in Italy.) Some obsidian (volcanic glass) knives still have some organic residues preserved from their last use. Thatch roofs are preserved even to the point of each of them having at least one mouse, and some roofs have up to six. Inside the structures, painted gourds, organic spindle whorls, and baskets are preserved. The stored grains are preserved inside fired clay vessels, even with two species of ants that got inside and were nibbling away. Gardens and agricultural fields are preserved, even with footprints of the farmers. Such extraordinary preservation of architecture, plants, and artifacts demands extraordinary efforts to conserve and preserve them. It would be an outrage to bring such wonderful items from their entombed past into the present and then give them a very short future by inadequate treatment.

CONSERVATION

The excavations are being conducted under a very strong ethic of conservation. There are three components to the conservation program: plants, artifacts, and architecture. Some plant remains are well-preserved in carbonized or direct forms and need little or no special treatment. They are submitted to biologists, mostly Salvadorans, for identification and interpretation.

Many plant remains are preserved as a cast. The fine-grained moist volcanic ash packed completely around the plants, whether they be trees,

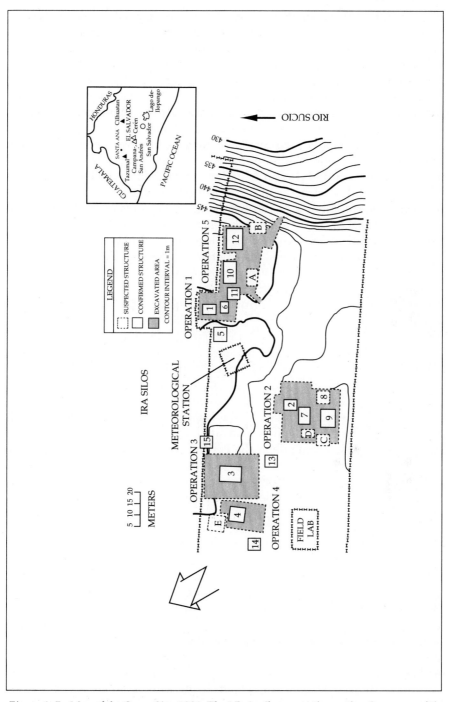

Figure 1–7. Map of the Ceren Site, 1991. The I.R.A. silos are to the north, where some of the village was destroyed by bulldozing in 1976. Known structures are indicated by solid lines and suspected structures by dashed lines. Suspected structures are ones for which indications of architecture have been found, but they have not been confirmed and excavated yet.

maize plants, or smaller items. The plants decomposed, leaving a hollow space. When we excavate within a meter or so of the previous ground surface, we do so with exceptional care, looking for hollow spaces. When a cavity is encountered, we look into it with a fiber optic proctoscope, as it is ideal for looking into small, dark spaces.[4] It conducts light through a fiber optic bundle to the end, to illuminate the cavity. A coherent bundle of optical fibers transmits the image to the eye of the archaeologist, to identify what made the void and to determine the best mode of preservation. Although some plant voids are merely branches from trees blown in during the early blasts of the eruption, many are planted and tended species. A specialist from the National Museum of Health and Medicine, Sean Murphy, trained us in the field in the use of dental plaster to fill the voids and preserve the plant as a plaster mold. Dental plaster has two advantages: It hardens to a very tough substance, and it preserves minute details. Often it even picks up the original colors of the decayed plants, and we have cast maize plants, many different seeds, trees, manioc plants, agave plants, maize cobs and ears of maize, storage cribs, front doors of structures, and many other organic materials.

Architectural conservation was assisted by the consultation of numerous specialists from the U.S., Guatemala, Italy, and Peru, and a major effort of architectural conservation continued simultaneous to the excavations. The Ministry of Education hired a permanent crew of 14 workers, under the supervision of Victor Manuel Murcia, to do architectural conservation. They established what could possibly be called an archeological "first" by consolidating the walls of Structure 4 before they were excavated. When only the very top surface of the walls was found, and before the ash from the sides of the walls was excavated, the conservation crew was able to insert straight wooden poles called "varas" into the walls. The prehistoric varas were virtually identical to the ones we inserted. Had we not replaced the varas, the walls would be too weak to stand up to even a moderate earthquake. Architectural conservation was done on all buildings as excavations continued.

With the assistance of Harriet Beaubien, Conservation Analytical Laboratory, Smithsonian Institution, a field laboratory for object conservation was established. Both nonperishable and perishable artifacts were treated, including ceramics, chipped stone, groundstone, baskets, painted gourds, cloth, twine, seeds, thatch, bone, antler, and other materials. Beaubien is creating a reference collection of the pigments used at Ceren, particularly those used on small, fragile artifacts and other special applications. Each is being characterized chemically.

CEREN HOUSEHOLDS

Ceren households hid all of their fine obsidian prismatic blades when they were not in actual use, generally in the roofing thatch but occasionally tucked into a crack in a wall. That probably was done to protect the edges as well as to protect children from being cut. The Ceren site is the only one I know of in Latin America that is so well-preserved we can learn how people did "child-proofing" of houses in prehistory. Valued and fragile items, such as polychrome pots or "donut" stone mortars, were often placed on top of adobe walls or with roofing for safekeeping. A total of 60 percent of the artifacts were kept off the floor, in elevated contexts.

In the U.S., the typical household lives in a single structure, be that a house, condominium, or apartment. Within that, functionally specific areas are demarcated by internal walls, separating bedrooms from the kitchen, living room, and other rooms. In contrast, Ceren residents constructed multiple buildings for specific functions per household. That also is in contrast to Lower Central America and northern Mesoamerica. In Lower Central America a household is encompassed by a single structure (cf. Lange and Stone 1984). In central Mexico, Oaxacan families constructed large rectangular buildings for multiple household activities (e.g. Whalen 1981), and internally subdivided them for particular activities. The same is true for Teotihuacan (Millon 1973) and later societies in the Basin of Mexico. Stone (1948) describes the Lenca earlier this century, in Honduras and El Salvador, living in single structures per family; most have only one room. The Chorti Maya of southeastern Guatemala (Wisdom 1940) presently construct a number of functionally specific buildings per household. The Classic Maya of Copan, the antecedents of the Chorti, constructed multiple structures per household (Webster and Gonlin 1988). The Kekchi Maya of Guatemala space families at least 30 meters from each other, and each family generally lives in a multiple-structure complex internally facing a patio (Wilk 1988).

Gerstle finds many architectural and space-use similarities with Ceren and the Maya at Copan. Given these similarities and differences, can we say if the Ceren residents were Maya or Lenca? The issue of cultural affiliation of Ceren residents is not clearly resolved, but architectural data would favor the Maya over the Lenca. However, in a frontier situation, with flux of goods and people, and acculturation occurring, it may be an oversimplification to expect Ceren residents to be clearly one or the other.

SUMMARY

The nature of volcanic preservation at the Ceren site provides an unusual opportunity to study southern Mesoamerican Classic Period households. The Laguna Caldera explosive eruption occurred with little or no warning, a characteristic of phreatomagmatic eruptions (magma in contact with water) of basaltic magmas. Hot, fluid basaltic magmas migrating upward caused negligible earthquakes. The site evidence is in agreement, as round-bottomed pots remained on top of flat adobe wall tops, and adobe platforms and walls were not cracked. However, when the magma struck water, probably from the Rio Sucio, a series of violent steam explosions occurred. Structures, artifacts, plants, animals, and evidently people were enveloped by hot (almost 100 degrees C) moist clouds of volcanic ash and gasses that were moving between 50 and 200 kilometers per hour. The eruption rapidly buried the site under five to seven meters of volcanic ash, sealing it from the factors of natural and human disturbance mentioned above. It also preserved organic materials, often to the cellular level. Those include palm and grass roofing thatch, roofing support posts and beams, grains in storage as well as the insects and field mice consuming them, and organic residues in food serving vessels and on food grinding and cutting implements. Sixty percent of household possessions were stored in elevated, protected contexts. Those contexts most frequently included wall tops, rafters, elevated shelves, and tables.

2
The Theoretical Framework: Household Archaeology

If research is to be more than merely collecting miscellaneous facts, curiosities, or flashy items to put in a museum display case, it must be done in a theoretical framework. A theoretical framework gives us a system of expected relationships, where a piece of data or an artifact can be related to a broader field. We can formulate hypotheses and test them, and thus assess them by finding them either supported or unsupported by the data. This allows an individual bit of data to be related to other artifacts and structures within an interpretive system. Possibly the most powerful and appropriate body of theory to help us in understanding the Ceren site is household archaeology. Household archaeology is a recently emerging subfield in anthropology that focuses on the group sharing the same residence and participating in certain common functions. In most cases this is a family, but there have been exceptions found in various parts of the world. For our purposes in this volume we assume the household is composed of a family, probably an extended family, until we encounter evidence to the contrary.

HOUSEHOLD ARCHAEOLOGY

Household archaeology focuses on the domestic coresidential group (Figs. 2–1, 2–2), and attempts to reconstruct activities regarding the functions of (1) *production* of food, artifacts, housing, etc., (2) *sharing and redistribution,* (3) *reproduction* of people in the biological sense, and their culture and society, and (4) *transmission* of goods and property to the next generation (Wilk and Rathje 1982). All four functions can be studied at a single point in time (synchronic) or through time on a processual basis (diachronic). The field of household archaeology is contributing to a "democratization" in Mesoamerican archaeology, as scholars shift from the elite emphasis of so many earlier projects. That traditional approach focused excavations in the centers of big sites, looking for the richly stocked tombs

Figure 2–1. A traditional Salvadoran family living on the slopes of Santa Ana Volcano. The mother (feeding baby), her sister (top left), and her five children are looking through the window of their kitchen, in mid-afternoon. The father is in the fields thatching a field house — see Figure 2–2.

of past rulers, fancy pyramids, elegant palaces, and the like. Fortunately, household archaeology begins from the "ground up" by investigating the functioning of prehistoric societies beginning with their basic building blocks, the household.

However, a major limiting factor inhibiting ample understanding and interpretation of prehistoric households is the quality of data, often due to poor preservation. The agents of natural disturbance, particularly strong in tropical climates, deleteriously affect most sites, particularly sites of commoners. The agents include erosion, solar radiation, bioturbation of flora and fauna, and other deranging variables interposing themselves between prehistoric activities and the archaeologist wishing to reconstruct them. As mentioned in Chapter 1, gradual abandonments allow people to remove their most valued possessions, and later people "mine" the site for usable materials. This introduces biases that are difficult to detect and measure unless cases such as Ceren are known where such factors were not operable.

Household archaeology is a rapidly developing subfield of anthropology. There is an expanding methodological and theoretical literature, primarily by ethnologists and ethnoarchaeologists. Ethnologists study contemporary functioning societies, ranging from the isolated hunting and gathering peoples in southern Africa to self-sufficient agricultural villages in the Amazon to industrialized communities in Europe. Household archaeology has roots in settlement archaeology (Willey et al. 1965, Chang 1968), in ethnoarchaeology (Kramer 1982, Wauchope 1938), ethnography (Wilk 1988, Wisdom 1940), and in affiliated social sciences (Arnould 1986). Settlement archaeology studies the distribution of residences of all levels of society and tries to understand how they functioned and related to each other. Ethnoarchaeology is the study of live, functioning societies by archaeologists to try to understand the role material culture (including architecture) plays in society. Thus, when archaeologists are trying to interpret prehistoric patterns, they are working from a more broad interpretive basis.

Household archaeology has changed in the past decade or so from a field with a few isolated practitioners to one with ethnographic sophistication, improving archaeological recovery techniques, and initiating an emerging corpus of appropriate method and theory (Netting, Wilk, and Arnould 1984, Wilk and Rathje 1982, Ringle and Andrews 1983, and Wilk and Ashmore 1988). Migratory hunter-gatherers deliberately maintain few material possessions and prefer multifunctional tools, because they have to carry everything when they relocate their base camps. In contrast, households in sedentary societies are immersed in material culture (Wilk and Rathje 1982), allowing for functional interpretations to reveal the nature of household activities. We have found that Wilk and Rathje's word

Figure 2–2. The father of the family placing thatch on a small field house in the cornfield, to be used as shelter in a sudden rainstorm. The grass thatch is tied to the roofing supports. Good thatch roofing was essential to the adobe architecture of Ceren. The other man (left) is a friend who helped gather the wooden supports and thatching material. The two unrelated males are good friends and often help each other with various agricultural activities.

"immersed" to be appropriate for the Ceren household, as they had abundant personal possessions. But that should come as no surprise to us in this society, since when we move from one residence to another, we are faced with a morass of loaded cardboard boxes and a real hassle in moving them around.

The household is here defined as the coresidential task-oriented social and adaptive unit intermediate in organizational level between the individual and the neighborhood. Behavior is spatially focused upon the house structure or structures and includes activities inside and outside the buildings. The behavioral emphasis exemplified by the major contributions of Netting, Wilk, and Arnould (1984) and Wilk and Ashmore (1988) are particularly appropriate to analyses and interpretations at Ceren. That does not mean that symbolic or mentalistic approaches cannot be done.

Symbolic studies often try to understand or speculate on why people do things on a deep level, and that can be difficult to test archaeologically. For instance, we would like to know why the dominant architectural orientation is 30 degrees east of north, but with rectangular structures that could also be 30 degrees south of east, or 30 degrees west of south, or 30 degrees north of west. Therefore, we do not know what their dominant direction was. Could they have been orienting on a celestial body, such as the rising or setting of the sun, moon, planet, constellation? Yes. Could they have been orienting on a feature of the natural environment, such as a prominent or sacred mountain? Yes. Could they have been organized somewhat arbitrarily by a central authority who was dictating the internal orientation of property? Yes. But what data can we collect to investigate these alternatives and try to see which is more likely? It is difficult to research these alternatives where there are no written records.

Following Adams (1981), households here are studied as "adaptive vehicles," as units which directly interrelate with their natural and social environments. As Laslett (1969) states, "a convincing case can be made out in favour of the household as the fundamental unit in pre-industrial ... society for social, economic, even educational and political purposes.... (The components) make up an intricate adaptive mechanism which we are only now beginning to understand." Households are localized and enumerable or countable (Arnould 1986), in contrast to families, which are kin-based and not necessarily localized (Netting et al. 1984). In other words, the household is the observable coresidential functioning unit, while occasionally families are split up and do not reside together. Therefore, strictly speaking, households are more suitable units for archaeological study than families.

According to Arnould (1986), all households share five spheres of activity: (1) *production*, including food, implements, vessels, and housing; (2) *pooling*, i.e. storage, distribution, maintenance, and curation of the common goods, including exchanges between households and communities; (3) *transmission* of information, knowledge, materials, and possessions, including inheritance and access rights to resources; (4) *reproduction* in biological and social-cultural senses, including the need to recruit spouses from outside the household and often outside the community; and (5) *co-residence membership*, with the activity areas of the household group revealing communal living and working.

Laslett's taxomony (1972) of households is sensitive to the household developmental cycle and is important when various households are being compared at a single point in time like at Ceren, or a single household is studied through time. At any point in time, a household is expected to be one of Laslett's following six types: solitaries (widowed or single individual), non-family (coresident siblings or unrelated members), simple family (married couple with or without children), extended family (extended laterally, upward, or downward in generations), multiple family, or indeterminate. As a household evolves, it can change from one type to another.

What is the boundary of a household, or what are the boundaries of a household? It is probably a mistake to ask this question in the singular, as there are a number of different kinds of boundaries. A structural boundary is the house construction itself, but a functional boundary includes the areas outside the walls and under the eaves, the adjacent activity areas, and outbuildings. Most Ceren structures excavated to date have more roofed area surrounding the structure than within the walls, providing roofed activity areas or walkways on all sides. Each household also had a number of specialized structures. A subsistence boundary is the edge of a garden or agricultural field. Field boundaries are discernable by changes in vegetation, hedgerows, etc. Also, Ceren residents often separated a field from a building by a walkway. An economic boundary encompasses the maximal geographic extent of commodities traded; this extended into Guatemala for jade, serpentine (used for a green pigment), and Ixtepeque obsidian, and the Pacific Coast for salt and shells. The sources of some other materials, such as hematite and cinnabar for red pigments, are yet unknown, but we do know that they were from volcanic sources and thus likely within a hundred kilometer radius or so. In this broader domain, household boundaries are expected to overlap considerably, and that overlap is an index of community and regional economic integration.

A chronic weakness of household archaeology in Mesoamerica has been the paucity of household-oriented excavations and publications. As Flannery (1976:13) noted, there existed "not a single published plan of a complete Early Formative [pre 1200 BC] house" anywhere in Mesoamerica. Classic and Postclassic houses, and occasionally households, are somewhat better known. Research in Oaxaca (Flannery 1976, Spencer 1981, Whalen 1981), south of Mexico City, has provided a strong stimulus to household archaeology elsewhere in Mesoamerica.

Researchers in Oaxaca provide comparative data and useful methods and concepts (Flannery 1976, Winter 1976). Winter (ibid:25) defines a "household cluster" as the houses, storage pits, graves, and associated ovens and middens. The household includes these features along with the activity areas inside and directly outside the house. Thus the term household includes the physical data and the interpretations of past human behavior of the functioning social unit. Oaxacan households varied somewhat in their features and were commonly spaced 20 to 40 meters apart. Winter estimates the individual Tierras Largas "household cluster" occupied 300 square meters, somewhat smaller than Ceren household areas.

Whalen (1981) excavated one of the best preserved houses yet found in Mesoamerica; most of the house floor and contact artifacts were preserved by the adding of fill for a new floor. Cooking and weaving were done on the "right side" of the house, as viewed from the doorway, probably by females. Archaeologists have disagreed about which artifacts were *in situ*, i.e. in their original position, which were somewhat misplaced, and which were inadvertent inclusions in construction fill. Spencer (1981) took a conservative approach and only included artifacts partially impressed into the floor. Parry (1987) argued for a more inclusive approach and included artifacts that seem to have been involved in intrahouse activities. It is not known what artifacts were in the house but were removed before the refurbishing buried some of the artifacts. Fortunately, the sudden burial by five meters of tephra at Ceren obviates these problems.

Although still small, the number of excavated southern Mesoamerican houses has increased in the past decade. Ringle and Andrews V (1983) recorded hundreds of Formative residences at Komchen, in northeastern Yucatan, and hundreds of other enigmatic smaller features of stone and soil, but excavated few. A range from small features to apparent housemounds to larger structures is representative of many Maya sites, and this makes it difficult to distinguish residences from outbuildings. Eaton (1975) has identified farmsteads (one-room stone-walled houses with fenced enclosures) and housemounds (raised platforms supporting perishable structures) in the Rio Bec area. Blake's excavations (1987) at Paso de la Amada, Chiapas, uncovered surprisingly large houses of an Early Formative chiefdom. Hammond et al. (1979) report on an early apsidal structure at Cuello, but the dating of the structure is not as early as originally claimed. It now appears to date to the Middle Formative.

Many significant advances in household archaeology in southern Mesoamerica have been accomplished at Copan and environs (Webster and Gonlin 1988), a major Maya site in western Honduras (Figure 1–1). Maya commoners, as agrarian "producers," had very basic housing, usually consisting of multiple small rectangular structures per household, sometimes on a platform, and active use of the "peripheral spaces" surrounding each structure. Structures were consistently aligned to the same azimuth, as at Ceren. Maya households in Copan proper had more substantial construction and more "ideal" Maya architecture, consisting of rectangular substructures with steps in front, terraces, and interior benches (ibid:186), when compared to houses in the periphery. Ceren architecture is more similar to the Copan core than to its agrarian periphery.

SUMMARY

Household archaeology in Mesoamerica has contributed to a process of democratization, as the elite-only bias to former research is broadening to include all components of society. The household is the coresidential group that shares many communal tasks. In most cases the household is a family, but not always. The household works together in activities of production, storage, distribution, curation, transmission, reproduction, and other functions. The household has been a neglected component of Mesoamerican studies but recently has become a mainstream component.

3

Multidisciplinary Studies: Geophysics, Volcanology, and Biology

It is unfortunate that we have to make such an effort to conduct multidisciplinary studies. It is a sign of the times, of the fragmentation of knowledge, of isolated disciplines in separate departments in universities, of funding agencies preferring "mainstream" research within specific fields. Disciplines as we now know them became formally separated in German universities a few centuries ago, and when universities in the U.S. and Canada began to be set up, they followed the German model. Thus we have separate departments of physics, chemistry, geology, biology, anthropology, psychology, and so forth, and they compete with each other for funding, faculty positions, and facilities.

Many research problems, particularly when they are narrowly defined, are quite appropriate to be investigated by highly specialized research teams from a single discipline, or even a small subfield within that discipline. However, many times important insights or worthwhile research opportunities are lost because of an overspecialized approach. We realized as early as 1978 that to understand what was happening at the Ceren site some 1400 years ago, we would have to broaden our perspectives rather than to become highly specialized as archaeologists. The other branches of science that have contributed fundamentally to the research effort are geophysics, volcanology, and biology. We will look carefully at their contributions in this chapter.

GEOPHYSICS

I turned to geophysics at the Ceren site more out of desperation than confidence. The problem was clear to me when I first saw the house in the bulldozer cut in 1978, buried under the five meters of volcanic ash (see

Figure 1–8). How could I find more buried structures? I certainly could not do so by following traditional archaeological survey procedures, of walking the present ground surface and looking for evidence of prehistoric artifacts or architecture. Imagine the frustration of walking a flat ground surface and knowing that there probably are a lot of structures, artifacts, and fields of supreme importance some 16 feet below your feet, but you cannot tell what or where they are.

Because the first structures were found by bulldozing, it was clear that more bulldozing could find more structures. However, the bulldozing would have to be random, on a massive scale, costing many tens of thousands of dollars per season, and generating immense amounts of backdirt (bulldozed loose waste volcanic ash). What could we do with all those tons of volcanic ash? Where could we put them? How do we move them? And, along another line, I had experienced some success and some failure in getting research proposals funded by the National Science Foundation (NSF), so I knew how well they had to be written. Because NSF receives so many proposals, yet they have a finite amount of money to award, most proposals are turned down. Often the rejection rate is 75 to 85 percent. I was certain that including a line item for some $30,000 of random bulldozing for a single season was sure to be the kiss of death for a proposal. Also, the term "random bulldozing" would inevitably strike the reader as far from an acceptable scientific procedure!

We needed a way to "see" through the volcanic ash layers to detect buried structures. However, there is no book or journal that one can consult on ways to look for Classic Period houses under five meters of volcanic ash. Rather, in desperation, I decided to take some samples of the ash and of the construction material back to the University of Colorado when I returned to Boulder in 1978. I knew that some unsuspecting geologist was about to have some plastic bags of ash and adobe architecture laid on his desk, but I had to find one that would not laugh me out of his office. Hence, I made some discrete enquiries of the geology departmental chair, who suggested that I talk with Dr. Hartmut Spetzler. He said that Hartmut had a reputation for enjoying challenges that he had not anticipated, and he enjoyed forays into fields outside his specialties of geophysics and tectonics.

Within an hour of my calling Hartmut to introduce myself and see if he would consider the problem, I was in his office with the samples and some photographs and stratigraphic drawings. He understood the problem immediately and began testing the samples in his laboratory. He needed to know the properties of the volcanic ash, because it forms the general matrix across the countryside. The first step is to know what the "background" is like before trying to find the buried buildings. To find the needle in the haystack you first need to measure the properties of the hay. Then Hartmut measured the properties of the construction material, which he would try to detect as an unusual feature, as an anomaly in an otherwise uniform field. He was encouraged by the porosity of the volcanic ash and the density of the earthen adobe construction. Also, the adobe construction material conducted electricity much better than the volcanic ash. We did the best we could to duplicate the moisture below the ground surface in the samples I had, but that was difficult, given the wet/dry season differences. We decided that most geophysical instruments would not be appropriate, due to size of target (three to five meters), depth of burial (about five meters down), nature of construction material, nature of the volcanic ash, and practicalities of shipping and running equipment in the field. We decided to try three instrument systems in the field, a portable seismograph, a ground-penetrating radar, and a resistivity instrument.

We wrote a proposal to the Committee on Research and Exploration of the National Geographic Society, and they funded it. So off to the Ceren site we went in the summer of 1979. Shipping the radar unit presented massive problems. The biggest problem we did not anticipate, which was that the U.S. government at the last moment prohibited us from shipping it out of the country. Some of the components, such as the instrumentation tape recorder and the radar, were so sophisticated that they might fall into the wrong hands. It took the intervention of some highly placed diplomats to finally get us permission to ship. We packed the radar equipment into its seven crates and took it to Stapleton Airport in Denver to be shipped to El Salvador. We then faced the difficulty of having all seven crates arrive there at the same time, undamaged, and then getting them through customs. We were greatly pleased and surprised that the airlines lost or delayed not a single crate. Customs in El Salvador was no problem, as the customs inspector had never seen anything remotely like this equipment and therefore had no grounds to be suspicious.

We began work in the field south of the bulldozed area in the summer of 1979, with the portable seismograph. Most of the remainder of this section on geophysical research is taken from the writing of Loker (1983) and Spetzler and Tucker (1989). The reader interested in more detail could consult either of these sources.

The seismograph records shock waves as they pass through the earth. Usually, a dynamite blast is used for the shock, and the waves pass through a few kilometers of rock and dirt. However, a dynamite blast five meters above a fragile Classic Period structure was clearly not appropriate, so we used a sledge hammer striking a steel plate set firmly on the ground as our energy source. It imparted plenty of seismic energy for our purposes, and the instrument detected the shock waves with an array of 12 geophones (sensitive microphones). We then looked for an anomaly. We expected, correctly, that a buried house floor would conduct the shock wave faster than the volcanic ash around it. The ash is less dense, somewhat like packed, coarse beach sand, and therefore was not as good a conductor. The shock point and the geophones can be laid out in an almost infinite number of patterns; we experimented until we found the best array for our target in its matrix. We did find some anomalies, and later checking has proven that some of them were in fact Classic Period structures, but many were not. The principal difficulty with this instrument was that we were pushing its

Figure 3–1. Ground-penetrating radar unit collecting data on subsurface stratigraphy. The sending-receiving antenna is attached to the rear of the oxcart. Inside the oxcart are the oscilloscope, instrumentation tape recorder, graphic recorder, gas-powered electric generator, and the geophysicist Hartmut Spetzler. Bill Loker is walking alongside, and Salvador Quintanilla is leading the oxen, named Senate and Cubano, along the grid line.

limits of accuracy, and we were getting equivocal results that were very difficult to interpret. It was made for detecting huge geological anomalies deep within the earth, not small buildings under shallow burial. Had we relied on seismicity alone, the geophysical research would have had very limited success.

Fortunately, the ground penetrating radar antenna, gas-powered electrical generator, oscilloscope, instrumentation tape recorder, graphic recorder, and all the other components, arrived simultaneously and undamaged. One problem we had was heat. The daytime highs were about 92 degrees F, and that coupled with the sunlight shining onto the instruments was enough to damage the data. We innovated a white cotton cloth cover, and that was enough to lower the temperature so the instruments could function (Figure 3–1). That gave us, inadvertently, a kind of Conestoga wagon look as we moved across the countryside. The instrument was developed to study permafrost melting by the Alaska Pipeline, and was used there attached to the tailgate of a pickup truck or suspended from a helicopter. All the data acquired using the pickup or helicopter had so much electrical interference from those vehicles that all data had to be digitized and computer manipulated, and that took months of tedious work. We avoided the need for that by employing an oxcart that has no

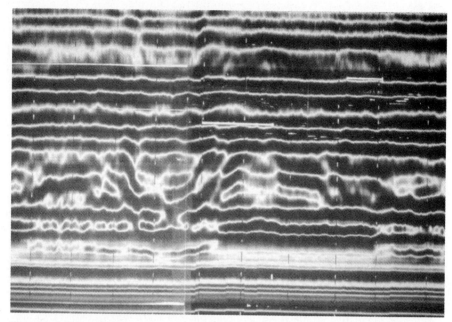

Figure 3–2. Raw data as it comes off the graphic recorder in the oxcart, as it moves across the surface. Each vertical line is five meters apart, and the depth recorded is about six meters. The black layers indicate a good radar reflector (such as a fine-grained dense tephra layer, a building floor, or the clay soil prior to Ilopango). A sizeable anomaly can be seen to the right of the center, with a good reflector buried by layers of tephra that bow up over it. This was later excavated and is now known as Structure 2, the domicile of Household 2.

electronic or moving metal parts. A trained team of oxen and driver can move at a very steady rate across a field in a straight line, along a string marked in five meter intervals. The clean data we obtained without digitizing was the envy of geophysicists at the Petrophysics division of the U.S. Geological Survey, who loaned us the instrument. They had never seen raw data so clean. They insisted that the next time we went to El Salvador we need to bring them back an oxcart, two oxen, and a driver.

A ground-penetrating radar has to be a very powerful unit, as it sends microwave energy deep into the soil and detects it as it is reflected back. The antenna sends and receives energy 50,000 times a second. The data can be seen on an oscilloscope in the oxcart as the equipment is moving across the ground surface. It is being recorded on special paper at the same time as the oxcart is moving, and one can see the subsurface stratigraphy unfurl (Figure 3–2). The black layers are strong reflectors, generally a dense volcanic ash layer overlain by a looser coarse layer. The anomaly visible to the right of center in Figure 3–2 shows the volcanic ash layers bowing up over a strong reflector. That strong reflector is the clay surface of a prepared house floor. This anomaly certainly looked to us like what we would expect, if it had been a building buried by the ash layers. However, it is a big step to go from a geophysical anomaly to a knowledge of what caused the anomaly.

The *Centro de Estudios Geotecnicos* (Geotechnical Studies Center) in San Salvador graciously loaned us a drill rig and crew to pull up a sample of the anomaly to see what it was. The drill rig uses a large impact hammer to pound a hollow pipe into the ground and then winch it back out again. The pipe is threaded and split, so when it is pulled up it can be opened and the stratigraphic layers studied and recorded. It turned out to be deliberate construction, and we considered the anomaly confirmed as a cultural feature.

Some anomalies detected with the radar have turned out to be natural, as the ash layers in one area had been eroded and redeposited during the eruption. Fortunately, other anomalies have been confirmed as cultural features. The anomaly shown in Figure 3–2 was drilled and confirmed as prehistoric construction. It was excavated in 1989 and is now known as Structure 2, the domicile for Household 2 (See Chapter 5). The ground-penetrating radar is able to detect the larger structures quite well, but the raw data are not sufficient to detect the smaller structures. A next step in geophysical research would be to digitize the data to see if they can discriminate the smaller structures from the background and perhaps even map the preexisting ground surface before the Laguna Caldera eruption. Of all the instruments used at Ceren, radar gives the fastest, most detailed results. Unfortunately, it is difficult to get the radar instrument to the field and back.

The third geophysical instrument used at Ceren is resistivity (Figure 3–3). The basic idea is that a house floor should conduct electricity better than the surrounding volcanic ash, because it is more dense and is made of clay that had been fired. Also, it would retain more moisture than the sloping layers of volcanic ash just outside a structure. Thus, we expected that the resistivity, or resistance to electricity passing, would increase near a structure, then decline right over the structure, and then increase on the other side of the structure. Our expectations were actually borne out by the results, although there are many other factors contributing to resistivity variation. In individual resistivity traverses we found interesting M-shaped anomalies (Figure 3–4), and when we entered our data into our laptop portable computer with 3-dimensional software, we saw interesting double and triple peaks popping out in various areas. Later explorations with the core drilling rig of the *Centro de Estudios Geotecnicos* indicated that all the strong double-peaked anomalies were sizeable prehistoric structures. Structures 2, 3, and 4 were so detected. Resistivity, however, does not have the sensitivity or resolution to detect the smaller structures.

The geophysical research directed by Hartmut Spetzler has been very successful in detecting the larger buried structures. Therefore we excavated around the larger structures to find the smaller ancillary structures that make up the household group. We have thus been able to avoid the waste of funds and time in random bulldozing, or, more likely, the rejection of a research proposal asking for large amounts of money to pay for random bulldozing.

Figure 3–3. Kayla Sheets and Hartmut Spetzler conducting resistivity survey in a sugar cane field. The instrument at their feet records the resistance of the subsurface to the passage of electricity; rods to their left and right are the electrodes (not visible in this photograph).

There is an unfortunate reason why it may become more important to archaeology in the future to be able to employ geophysical instruments to detect deeply buried archaeological sites. The amount of looting of archaeological sites in El Salvador, like most countries of the world, is very discouraging. People illegally excavate sites looking for polychrome pots, jade artifacts, and other things that they can either add to their personal collections or sell to make money. The result is the destruction of archaeological sites; more than half of the sites in El Salvador are scarcely worth excavating because they have been so badly looted. Unless looting is halted soon, and that prospect seems unlikely, we are facing a situation where only the few carefully protected sites, or sites deeply buried, will be worth expending the funds and effort necessary to excavate them. The deeply buried sites require special instrumentation, and we are trying to develop some of that for the future.

VOLCANOLOGY: INSTANT BURIAL, FREEZING A MOMENT IN TIME

Had Laguna Caldera not erupted and the structures in the Ceren site been abandoned under usual circumstances, the Ceren site would not be very special. It would be much like the common Classic Period sites dotting the Central American landscape. If the thatch roofs are not maintained, they deteriorate badly in a year or two. Once the roof is gone, the rain and sun rapidly "melt" the adobe architecture. Not only do the structures deteriorate to virtually nothing, the more important artifacts would have been hauled off, leaving only trash, and archaeologists excavating there would have found a greatly diminished data base. Fortunately for us, but unfortunately for Ceren residents at the time, Laguna Caldera erupted suddenly and buried the site. It is logical that because the eruption was so critical for preservation, it is important to understand the nature of the eruption.

A number of volcanologists, or geologists specializing in volcanic eruptions, have contributed to our understanding of the eruption. They include Virginia Steen-McIntyre, William Hart, Richard Hoblitt, and Dan Miller. Our present knowledge is summarized in Hoblit (1983) and Miller (1989). This section on volcanology is largely taken from those sources, and the reader is encouraged to consult them for more detail.

The eruption began when an upwardly moving column of very hot basaltic magma came into contact with water, probably the Rio Sucio. It probably occurred near to, or under, where Laguna Caldera Volcano is today. Prior to the eruption there was no volcano there, only a tranquil valley with the river flowing down the middle. However, the magma contacted water and instantly vaporized it, causing a massive steam explosion. That initiated a lateral blast, called a pyroclastic ("pyro" means fire, and "clastic" means broken) surge, that consisted of hot gasses, water vapor and

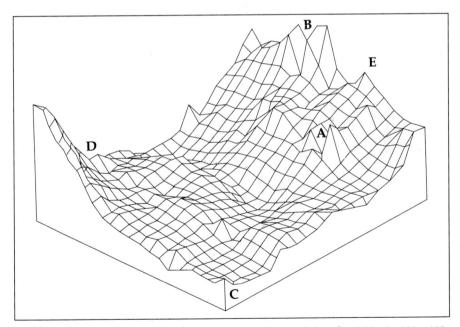

Figure 3–4. Each of the resistivity measurements, at 5 meter intervals within the 100 x 100 meter grid, are entered into the computer in the field, resulting in a 3-d plot. The anomaly known as "A," when excavated, is now known as Structure 2, and the anomaly "B" is known as Structure 3. Structure 4's anomaly is just beginning to the left of "B." Anomaly "C" seems to be natural, and "E" and "D" have yet to be explored.

steam, and fine-to-coarse fragments of magma that were blasted through the air as tephra. The first layer of deposit is known as Unit 1. The various layers of the eruption are alternations of pyroclastic fall and pyroclastic surge phases of the eruption. The more coarse-grained and darker fall beds, such as Units 2 and 4, are composed of pieces that fell vertically onto the site through the air. The larger pieces fell quite hot, while the more fine-grained layers, such as Units 1 and 3, fell at a cooler temperature. They were about the boiling temperature of water, 100 degrees Celsius, and generally were propelled into the site laterally. As pyroclastic surges, they had velocities between 50 and 200 kilometers per hour. The overall duration of the entire eruption was days or a few weeks. We call it the Laguna Caldera eruption, and indeed it seems that a majority of the tephra came from there, but it is likely that other materials came from other portions of the active fault or fissure. The larger lava bombs evidently were not direct airfall, being blasted up into the air and then settling down vertically. Rather, they followed ballistic trajectories, long parabolas, and arrived at high velocities. They did considerable damage when they hit structures or artifacts. Often they exploded because of the release of volcanic gases that were trapped inside their cooling crusts as they traveled through the air. A big lava bomb more than a half meter in diameter landed right on top of a fired clay storage vessel in Structure 6 and blasted it into hundreds and hundreds of tiny fragments. Marilyn Beaudry-Corbett, the project ceramicist, has spent many hours trying to put that jigsaw puzzle back together again. We do not know if it contained anything before the eruption, as it was blasted by the lava bomb.

The first phase of the Laguna Caldera eruption, which deposited Unit 1, was composed of pyroclastic surge beds. The particles are small and "fire-broken" because they were very hot and in contact with water, which fractured them to tiny pieces. The Unit 1 deposit generally is 20 to 30 centimeters thick. Hot steaming deposits of fine-grained Unit 1 tephra blasted through the site and packed around walls, trees, and on top of thatch roofs. The turbulence of Unit 1 arriving was sufficient to tip over some pots, knock some artifacts off of wall tops and from rafters, and detach some parts of adobe cornices of buildings. Tephra is the generic term for all kinds of volcanic ash, lapilli, bombs, and so forth, that travel through the air, in contrast to lava, which stays on the ground. Most of the buildings and roofs survived this stage of the eruption, and thus people inside of buildings would have been protected enough to have survived Unit 1. However, a person in an exposed position (for example, not inside a substantial building) would have only a minute or two to live, as death would soon follow the first breath of this noxious cloud.

This type of eruption generally gives little warning, so it is likely that it caught Ceren residents by surprise. We have been looking for any evidence of earthquakes that might have occurred just before, or during the eruption, and found evidence to the contrary. Had there been significant earthquakes, we would see some cracking of the adobe architecture, and the round-bottomed ceramic vessels that had been stored on top of flat wall tops and shelves would have tumbled to the floor. They had not.

We are also accumulating information on the time of day, or night, when the eruption occurred. So far, the bulk of the evidence indicates an eruption that began at night, as most artifacts seem to be "put away" from their locations of daytime use. The cooking pot had been removed from the hearth, and the fire had been allowed to die down. The meal, probably dinner, had been served, but not all the vessels had been washed, as we found their "dirty dishes" in Structures 2 and 4. However, it was not late at night, since the sleeping mats were still wrapped up and stored in the rafters and had not been spread on the benches for sleeping. Therefore, based on the evidence collected so far, we feel the eruption began in the late evening.

Unit 2 represents the second phase. We have not yet been able to devise a means to estimate the time between the end of Unit 1 and the beginning of Unit 2. If it was significant, such as an hour or more, there would have been time for people who were protected from Unit 1 by buildings to flee before Unit 2 arrived. Unit 2 varies from five to 15 centimeters in thickness and is a lapilli (pea-sized particles) and block (large pieces) airfall deposit. The larger pieces are of juvenile magma, and Hoblitt (1983) was able to determine that they were hotter than 575 degrees Celsius.[5] The largest pieces were so big they followed ballistic trajectories, while the others were direct vertical airfall. Some lava bombs, which fell during most Units, were almost a meter in diameter and were tremendously destructive when they fell. Many exploded on impact, and most left bomb sags or bomb craters. It must have seemed that war had broken out all of a sudden. As the larger hot lava bombs hit thatch roofs, the roofs caught fire and burned intensely. Very few roofs failed during Unit 1 or 2 deposition; most failed during Unit 3 emplacement. Only the thin roof of Structure 11, the kitchen, failed during Unit 1.

We know that there was very little time between the ending of Unit 2 and the beginning of Unit 3, for the following reasons. A thatch roof burns rapidly, so had there been as much as a quarter hour between Unit 2 ending and 3 beginning, the thatch roofs would have burned and collapsed. However, virtually all the thatch roofs at Ceren failed when Unit 3 was arriving and accumulating on top of the roofs, overloading them at the same time that the burning was weakening them from below. Thus, roof collapse was due both to burning weakening the roofs from below and the accumulating overburden above.

Unit 3 is a thick layer, two-thirds to three-quarters of a meter thick, and like Unit 1 it is composed of a series of pyroclastic surges that were blasted laterally by steam explosions. This was a time of intense surge activity from the volcano, and thick wedges or ramparts of material accumulated in drifts on sides of walls toward the volcano and on downwind sides after the roofs failed. Often these ramparts served to reinforce walls and aided them in resisting volcanic blasts from later phases of the eruption. Most arrived as pasty gobs of hot tephra the temperature of boiling water.

Some ballistic blocks continued to fall during Unit 3. Unit 3 arrived with considerable horizontal force, being propelled by turbulent winds traveling between 50 and 200 kilometers per hour. Unit 3, as with Unit 1, was fine-grained and moist, and so it packed around plants, poles, trees, and other organic materials and helped preserve them.

Units 4 through 14 are an alternating series of vertically deposited airfall beds and pyroclastic surge deposits that largely repeat the sequence of Units 1 through 3 described earlier. It is likely that they represent a few days in total elapsed time, as this type of volcanic eruption is generally short-lived. The fact that standing walls of buildings and elevated plat-forms acted as barriers and trapped tephra both upwind and downwind assists us as we try to find buried structures with geophysical instruments. The bulging of the tephra layers is detected directly with radar or indirectly with resistivity. Even the smallest structures create some humping or bulging of tephra layers. Fragile Structure 11, with its floor barely above the surrounding ground surface and thin walls, created a bulge in Unit 3 that was visually detectable as we were excavating and assisted us in planning its excavation. The bigger structures create very large tephra bulges; the bulge from Structure 9 was visible as high up as Unit 10 and was more than eight meters wide. When we found a bulge of that magnitude, we were quite sure that there was a sizeable structure buried under it.

BIOLOGY

Preservation of organic materials is so great at Ceren that unusual measures have been taken to include biologists in the research program. Gardens have been found south of the bodegas in two households, and cornfields have been discovered associated with two households. Trees were discovered in various locations, including a line of trees to the west of Household 2. Branches commonly are found broken from their trees and blown into or near structures. Considerable amounts of palm and grass thatch were used in roofs, and poles and rafters supported them. Inside structures, large amounts of seeds were found in pots, in storage cribs, and hanging from rafters.

Manioc ("yuca") has been identified in the field but has yet to be confirmed by secure biological species identification. If this is manioc, it will be of considerable importance, as manioc is a root crop that produces a great amount of carbohydrates in a relatively small area, and it grows for years. It is a small tree, some two to three meters high, with long fat tubers growing underground, somewhat like huge potatoes. It is the tubers that are harvested and processed into food.

Maria Luisa Reyna de Aguilar, the director of the Jardin Botanico in San Salvador, identified a number of species at Ceren. Some were seeds being stored in structures, some were plants growing at the time of the eruption, and some were wood or thatch used for roofing before the erup-tion. Her report (Reyna 1991) was issued as an article in the informative bulletin series called *Pankia*. Because the annual plants were mature, she reasons that the eruption occurred during the middle of the rainy season, probably in August. Previously we had thought that the eruption was earlier, in June.

She identified maize (*Zea mays*) growing in various milpas, most of it mature, but some of it juvenile, perhaps the second planting of the rainy season. Some of the maize plants with mature ears were doubled over, which may have been done as a short-term storage in the field, as is still done in rural areas of Central America. The most extensive maize milpas have been found with Households 1 and 2. None of the maize, juvenile or mature, has beans interplanted. A garden with some 18 plants of "maguey" or "agave" (*Agave americana*) was discovered south of Structure 4. This is described in more detail later in this book.

A line of bromeliacea plants were growing just south of Structure 6. They were either "piñuela" (*Bromelia karatas*), which has an edible inforescence and is much used in atole, or "pita floja" (*Aeohmea magdalenae*) that was used much for string.

Clumps of flowering plants, called "macoyas," were found south of Structure 6, with ten to 20 plants of the same species in a tight group. These could be one of five species yet to be determined and could have been used for medicinal purposes.

Roofing support timber included laurel (*Cordia alliordora*), "caoba" (*Swietenia humilis*), "irayol" (*Genipa caruto*), "guarumo" (*Cecropia spp.*), "guachipilin" (*Diphysa robiniodes*), "flor de mayo" (*Plumeria rubra*), "quebracho" (*Lystoma divaricatum*), "huilihuishte" (*Karwinskia calderoni*), and "cedro" (cedar: *Cedrela odorata*).

Two species of "caña brava" were used as the vertical poles in bajareque walls, generally continued upward to assist in roof support. Both are in the bamboo family. They are *Gynerium sagittatum* that grows to 15 meters high and has a distribution from Mexico to Paraguay, and *Chusquea pitterii* that grows to 18 meters, has a ring of spines at each growth node, and has a distribution limited to Central America and Panama. It is possible that "huiscoyol" (*Bactris major*), a straight pole that grows in wet areas, was also used in bajareque walls.

Roofing thatch evidently was of the grass "tule" (*Cyperus canus*) or the palm "palma de sombrero" (*Sabal mejicana*). The latter has a distribution from Mexico into the northern portion of South America and remains the favored thatching material in ranchos in San Salvador.

Many species of seeds and other plant items were found stored inside of structures. They include maize, chiles, tomatoes, gourds "morros" (*Crescentia alata*), cacao (*Theobroma cacao*), beans (*Phaseolus spp.*) with at least three species represented based on size and shape variation, "achiote" (*Bixa orellana*) that is edible and is a pigment, squash "pepitoria" or "pipian" (*Cucurbita pepo*), "pacun" (*Sapindus saponaria*), "conacaste" (*Enterolobium cyclocarpum*), "jocotes" (*Spondias spp.*), and "guayabas" (*Psidium spp.*).

The following fauna also have been identified: dog, domestic duck, deer, freshwater snail "jute," olivella shells, and cowry shells.

The "jute" snail is important because it can only grow in very clean fresh water. The adjacent river is now so polluted that the snail is unable to survive there. One of the worst polluters is the Kimberly Clark factory, a paper mill three kilometers upstream from the site. Before the paper mill was built, local residents caught fish for dinner, swam in the stream, and washed their clothes in it. Kimberly Clark began dumping so many chemicals and acids in the river that all fish died out almost immediately after the plant began functioning. From a capitalist perspective it is good business for them, as they do not have to abide by Environmental Protection Agency standards. Local poor people have no political clout, and are powerless against big business. Hence, business profit margins may be better than if they had to operate a clean plant and exhibited some respect for the environment and concern for people living nearby. People still do bathe in the river but complain of skin burns and foul odors. They have no alternative. People still do wash their clothes in the river, but they note how they do not become clean, and they don't last very long. The river is appropriately named the "Rio Sucio," the "dirty river." The present living conditions in Central America contrast sharply with those in the past.

SUMMARY

Our project's use of scientists from other disciplines is not merely an attempt to be "trendy" and jump on the multidisciplinary bandwagon. To put it directly, the project could not operate without successful geophysics. How would we find structures buried under five meters of volcanic ash? Random bulldozing simply is not acceptable for a number of reasons. Finding buried structures, first as anomalies with the radar and resistivity instruments, and then determining their nature with the core drill rig, was an essential first step in organizing the archaeological research.

The eruption of Laguna Caldera Volcano was not a simple blast that deposited a layer of uniform volcanic ash across the countryside. Rather, it had at least 14 distinct phases, and multiple vents along a fissure may have been involved. It appears that the larger lava bombs came from less than a kilometer away. The grain size, original moisture content, temperature, and velocity of the volcanic ash deposits had clear impacts on the structures, their roofs, artifacts, food grains, plants, trees, and other things in the area. The trained eyes of volcanologists have been essential to revealing the phases of the eruption and their effects on the site.

Biologists have helped in identifying the flora and fauna of the site, which was an essential first step in understanding how people adapted to their landscape. Because our excavations of the Ceren site are just beginning, I would guess that we have found and identified well less than half the species of wood, seed, fruits, nuts, medicinal plants, and other plant species that they used. In spite of that, I think it is impressive—the range of foods they consumed, the variety of woods they used in construction, and their adapting to the tropical environment in a way that did not lead to environmental degradation.

4

The Ceren Site: Household 1

Of all the households excavated at Ceren, Household 1 is the best known, as four separate structures have been excavated, along with outside activity areas, a kitchen garden, and a maizefield (Figure 4–1). The building of multiple structures for a single household contrasts with our housing pattern, where a single building and roof are constructed. Then, many of our specialized activities receive their own partitioned space within the building, including the kitchen, dining and living room, bedrooms, and storage areas. There may have been a number of reasons for their building separate structures for specific functions at Ceren. One may have been cultural tradition. The Chorti Maya Indians who now live 100 kilometers north of Ceren have, for as long as they can remember, built separate structures for particular functions, and they state that "es costumbre" ("it is customary") as a reason. Another is practicality in thatch roofing. Many of the structures had roofs that were in the range of five by five meters, and if they had to combine all intramural spaces of a household under a single roof, it would have been extremely large thus it would have been more vulnerable to wind damage than a set of smaller, lower roofs.

The four structures of Household 1 are separated by two to four meters (Figure 4–2). The closest structures are less than two meters apart, meaning that the thatch of their roofs were almost touching. There was only a short gap for rain to drain into and run away and sunlight and air to enter. The men's workshop, Structure 5, was almost four meters away from the others, perhaps deliberately located farther away.

THE DOMICILE (STRUCTURE 1)

Structure 1 is now known to have been the principal family building of the complex. For lack of a better term, this is called the domicile to avoid the awkward but descriptive phrase of "the eating, sleeping, and daytime activity structure of the household."

The northern end of Structure 1 was bulldozed away in 1976, when the platform for the massive storage silos was being prepared. Originally we feared that a substantial portion of the building was demolished, but it now

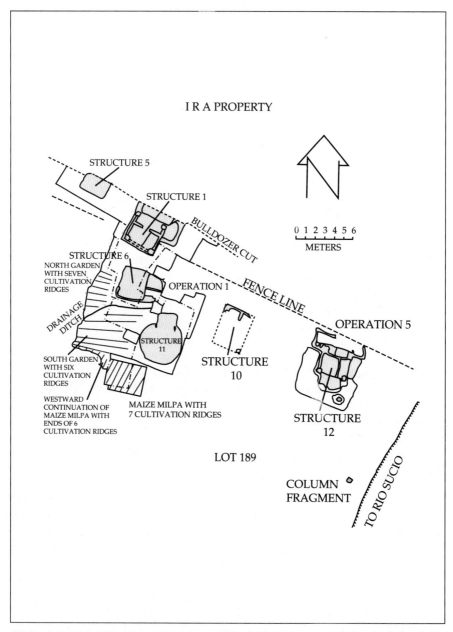

Figure 4–1. Map of Operation 1, known as Household 1. Structure 1 is the domicile, where the family ate, slept, made pottery and cotton thread, and stored some implements and food. Structure 5 is the male workshop. The storehouse is Structure 6, opening to the east. The kitchen, Structure 11, opens to the north. The north garden and the area around Test Pit 2 was all in maize cultivation, with plants up to about 20 centimeters high. The south garden had at least four different species growing; note how field ridges line up with the dominant architectural orientation.

Figure 4–2. Artist's reconstruction of the domicile (Structure 1) of Household 1 in the center, with the workshop on the right (Structure 5) and the storehouse on the left (Structure 6).

looks like a very small portion was destroyed (Beaudry and Tucker 1989). Two other areas of structures, likely household complexes, were completely destroyed by the bulldozing. They were located about 50 meters northeast and 100 meters northwest of Structure 1. All we have regarding those structures are informants' accounts of their approximate locations and descriptions. Informants' accounts of human bodies seated on the floor of the destroyed northern portion of Structure 1, as reported by Zier (1983: 123), are not considered reliable.

As with virtually all buildings excavated at Ceren, Structure 1 is oriented 30 degrees east of magnetic north. As mentioned above, we do not know if they were thinking north, or were really aligning 30 degrees south of east, nor do we know how or why they were following this alignment. In any event, the fact that household and special purpose buildings and crops generally aligned to the same orientation is an indication of an authority or order above the household, something that we should expect within the complex, hierarchical society that lived in the Zapotitan Valley 1400 years ago.

Most structures at Ceren followed standardized construction procedures. A description of the construction of Structure 1 will suffice for all buildings, unless otherwise noted. The first step in construction was to dig down through the Ilopango volcanic ash to the pre-eruption soil and begin piling that soil into a low mound that was slightly longer and wider than the building to be constructed. Evidently that was for drainage, so rain falling off the edge of the roof would run away from the structure. Successful drainage is essential for earthen architecture in a wet, tropical environment. The clay was mixed with some pieces of grass, as a kind of tempering material, so that it would not crack when it dried. That is similar to making pottery from clay, as it too needs temper so it will not crack during drying or firing.

After completing the low mound, the formal construction of the floor of the building and the platform began. The platform was built with vertical sides and right-angle corners, and its top formed the floor of the building. Building platforms were quite precisely rectangular; construction was done to less than 5 percent variation in north versus south walls, or east versus west walls. The platform was made of clay from the same source and mixed with grass. After it dried, a large fire was built all around and over it, oxidizing and hardening it like a large fired brick. Then, four solid adobe columns, about 1.5 meters high, were mounted at corners or at ends of planned walls. Vertical poles were placed about every 15 centimeters along the east, south, and west sides of the platform and connected with horizontal sticks. The same clay and grass mixture was then packed on the inside and outside to make a smooth, reinforced adobe wall to about 1.5 meters in height. The wall is about 15 centimeters thick. This kind of internally reinforced earthen wall construction is called "bajareque," and it is very earthquake resistant. It is horizontally and vertically reinforced, and it takes a strong earthquake to crack it. It takes an even stronger earthquake to dislodge pieces, and those pieces are small, being formed by the intersections of the horizontal and vertical reinforcements. Not only are the vertical sticks anchored down into the platform, but they are tightly tied together by horizontal roofing beams. Thus, the walls are tightly integrated at the bottom and the top and are also reinforced within the wall itself.

After completing the walls and roofing framework, palm thatch was placed on top. A thatch roof can "breathe," and it needs a fairly strong angle to enable it to wick the water away. Other structures at Ceren had grass thatch; there is little difference in effectiveness or duration. Both last about four years and then have to be redone.

The vertical poles in the bajareque walls continue upward above the clay-daubed part of the wall to support the roof. Thus, they leave an opening above the clay wall that does not diminish privacy and allows light to enter and air to circulate. The poles were tied firmly to the roof to make a tightly integrated and reinforced structure. The bajareque walls and columns were not structurally interconnected directly to each other. However, they did not need to be, as long as the roof remained intact as the overarching network giving strength. Thus, Structure 1 could successfully withstand even a major earthquake. What Ceren architectural planners did not envision was the Laguna Caldera eruption, with lava bombs hotter than 575 degrees Celsius, which caught the roofs on fire. Roof failure eliminated the structural reinforcement from above, and many bajareque walls collapsed.

Area 1 is the original front porch of the structure, enclosed by bajareque walls on the east, south, and west. The original step up into the

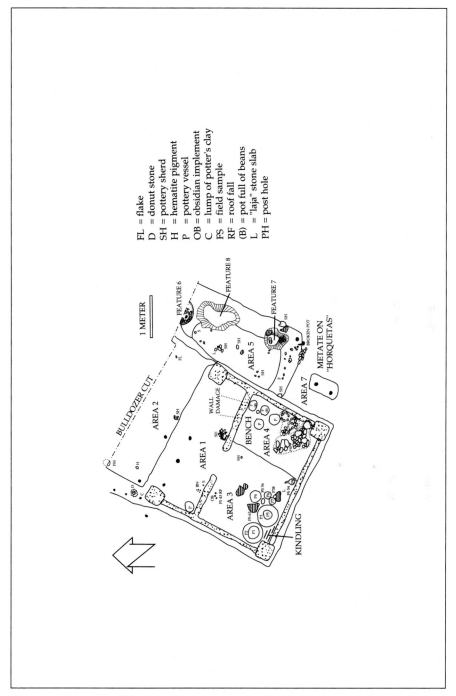

Figure 4–3. Map view of Structure 1, the domicile, with artifacts. After it was constructed, the roof was extended over Area 5 and the floor was prepared for a work area, probably for females.

domicile is located under the words "Area 2" of Figure 4–3. That step was covered up by the remodeling that created Area 2 as an extension of the front porch. It apparently was used as a multipurpose space, since a pot and a spindle whorl (for making cotton thread) were found in one corner, and a crudely made miniature pot and 20 rounded potsherds (broken fragments from various pots) were found together in another corner. The miniature pot and the 20 sherds may have been a child's playthings. Their numerical system probably was a base 20, based on ethnographic evidence, and the child may have been learning to count.

Area 2 is the lower porch formed by covering over the step and extending the floor northward. It more than doubled the original porch, but the northernmost edge was removed by the bulldozing of 1976, which likely carried away the front step. The porch was open on three sides. A pottery working area was found on its western side, with a prepared lump of clay still bearing the fingerprints of the pottery maker. The clay matches the clay of the utilitarian (undecorated) pottery of the household, according to detailed studies done by Southward and Kamilli (1983). They conducted petrographic studies, which broke the samples down into their component minerals and elements. The clay lump and the utilitarian pottery are sufficiently similar to have derived from the same clay source and probably indicate manufacture in the household. The only chipped stone artifact found in the north half of the house was an andesite flake with edge abrasion characteristic of pottery smoothing. The Copador and Gualpopa polychrome pottery from this household was ornate, decorated pottery and was sufficiently different from the pottery known to have been made in the household that it is believed to have come from a different source. It probably was manufactured somewhere else, perhaps obtained at a marketplace, and brought into the household readymade.

Area 3 is the fairly sizeable inner room, with four square meters of surface. The floor was kept largely clear of artifacts, as befits a high-use zone. An obsidian prismatic blade was found in the roofing thatch. It, as with almost all other prismatic blades in usable condition in the site, was stored up in the roofing thatch. I believe this is to protect cutting edges and children. The cutting edges were valuable, as the obsidian had to be imported all the way from Ixtepeque Volcano in Guatemala, some 80 kilometers to the northwest. A fairly high degree of skill was needed to manufacture the obsidian, and it probably required an occupational specialist. Both of these factors mean that it was expensive; in other words, that quite a bit of something such as maize had to be exchanged for it. Also, a recently manufactured obsidian edge is very sharp, sharper than any steel edge, and it would do considerable damage to some young child who crawled across it. Storage in the soft roofing thatch protected the obsidian knives and the children.

Two large storage jars were resting on the floor in Area 3, against the back wall, with two smaller vessels on top of their rims acting as caps. One small spherical jar was found on the floor, missing its rim. This is one of many vessels found at Ceren that had been partially broken and thus was not complete but still was being used. In many cases the partial breakage made the initial function inappropriate, and the function shifted. Usually we think, as archaeologists, that pots are complete, or they were broken and thrown away. However, some pots were nearly complete and still in use. Some big pots were broken, but some large sherds were salvaged and used as informal large plates. Also, one of the more ingenious re-uses of pottery involved saving the handles of large, broken storage vessels and mounting them in clay walls during building construction. They functioned as hangers or anchors to tie a variety of things. All adobe or bajareque doorways had four ex-jar handles mounted inside, two at the top and two at the bottom, to tie the wooden stick door shut.

Many different parts of vessels were retained for use after the original vessel broke. Sometimes when part of the rim or the entire neck broke, the rest of the pot would be saved and used. Or when a large pot broke, big sherds were used somewhat like large plates. Vessel handles were used as described above.

One of the seven pots on the floor, tucked away against the back wall, was used to store valuable items probably belonging to a female. It contained a spindle whorl probably used for making cotton thread, a miniature metate used for grinding red paint, three small cylinders of red paint, and pieces of sea shell.

Area 4 is the elevated solid adobe bench that probably was used by the family as a bed at night, by unrolling mats to make it comfortable. During the daytime the mats were rolled up and stuck up in the rafters, and the bench probably was where the family ate and engaged in other familial activities. A cornice, or overhanging "bar" of adobe, was added as decoration to the western edge of the bench. It seems that cornices were becoming quite popular, as they were used for architectural decoration of many buildings at Ceren, but this is the only one in Household 1. It was not very well constructed or connected to the bench, as the eruption dislodged much of it. Four pots were on the bench in its northeastern corner, two of which were full of small beans. The other two were empty but might have contained a liquid. The other artifacts in the area were suspended from the roofing. That included large amounts of chile peppers that probably were hanging in bunches. Above the chiles were two partial ceramic vessels, one being the lower half of a very large storage vessel one-half meter in diameter. This is an example of the salvaging of partial broken vessels and shifting their use. The other is a partial polychrome bowl.

Area 5 was added to the structure after it was built. The roof extended the roofline already established, so the roof must have been very low, especially at the eastern edge. That probably accounts for the sunken center and the low sitting bench with a woven mat around the outside. It was a craft area, judging by the spindle whorl on a spindle for making cotton thread, some broken pots, and an obsidian flake. A "donut stone," which is a round disk with a hole in the middle, was found in a most curious position. The bajareque wall that divided Areas 1 and 5 fell over Area 5, along with the donut stone still mounted on its stick. These artifacts have been the subject of considerable controversy, with some people arguing that they were religious and functioned as scepters. Others argued that they were military and served as club heads. Others thought they were agricultural and functioned as digging stick weights. That does seem to be the function of this one. As we will see later, these donut stones had more than one function, proving that it has been a basic error to ask the question, "what was their function?"

The general area between Structure 1 and the family's storehouse ("bodega"), or Structure 6, was very interesting. A zone closest to Structure 1 was kept clean of artifacts and served as a walkway, covered by the thatch roof eaves. However, Area 7 was a food-grinding area, as evidenced by a metate (bottom grinding stone) found on the forked sticks ("horquetas") that elevated it to waist level. A few sherds, pots, and a little human figurine head were stored on the rafters above the grinding area.

THE STOREHOUSE OR "BODEGA" (STRUCTURE 6)

The storehouse was built on a shallow platform, elevated only 20 to 30 centimeters above the surrounding area. The platform is square, measuring about 3.2 meters on a side. The two side walls and the back wall were variants on bajareque. The vertical poles extended up to support the roof, but only the bottom ten to 35 centimeters were adobe-coated. Hence, it was very open to air circulation. Curiously, the eastern wall received full bajareque treatment, with adobe coating up to 1.8 meters in height, and a well-made doorway. That is higher than most walls anywhere in Ceren excavated to date. The building gives me a vague feeling of a false front building on a movie set, with so much effort in the front wall. It is possible that the building was being renovated, but they had completed only the east wall when the eruption struck.

The Household 1 bodega shares some characteristics with the other two bodegas, yet it differs in others. As with the other two, it was loaded with pottery vessels, many with food. Each bodega had about a half dozen mice in the thatch roof. All bodegas are square in groundplan and are located just south of the domicile building. However, there are a number of ways in which this bodega was different. It was set up for grain grinding inside the structure, with a metate set up on the horquetas. It had a duck tied to the back wall. It had very insubstantial walls, except for the east wall with the doorway, and a very low platform.

Beaudry and Tucker (1989) subdivide the bodega into four areas (Figure 4–4), and I shall follow their subdivision, as there is some clustering of artifacts. The entrance was on the east, and the area inside the door extending most of the way across the structure was maintained largely free of artifacts, as an access corridor. The first area Beaudry and Tucker discuss

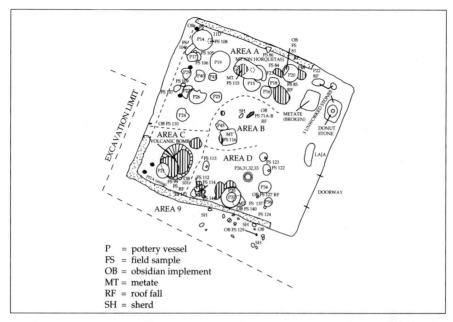

Figure 4–4. The storehouse (bodega) of Household 1 (Structure 6). A volcanic bomb landed on some pots in Area C and smashed them into tiny pieces into the floor. Most pottery vessels were stored along the south or the north walls. A metate was mounted on horquetas in Area A. A duck was found in Area D, with its leg tied with string to a pole of the south wall.

is the northern segment, which has the greatest number and variety of artifacts of all four areas. There is dense artifact storage of pottery vessels (some loaded with seeds), hammerstones, obsidian artifacts, and a mano and metate. The metate was mounted up on the horquetas and was almost identical to the other two horqueta-mounted metates in Household 1 in its minimal use and its low height above the floor. It was only about 50 centimeters above the floor, indicating that a short female was the principal maize grinder of the family. A mano and a metate are a matched pair that wear together to ensure a tight fit, and this metate's mano was found a meter to the west, on the floor. This is not in a use position, and the floor around the metate was cluttered with utilitarian pottery, so this was not a primary grinding area but a backup area. It would take only a few minutes to get it into grinding condition by moving some pots out of the way and recovering the mano.

The northern part of the building had 18 ceramic vessels, ten of which had been damaged during use but had not been discarded. Damage entailed the breaking of part of a rim or the like, but the majority of the damaged pots retained most of their storage capacity. There was a surprisingly high number of fancy polychrome pottery: five vessels. One pot had an ingenious way of filling in a small pencil-sized hole. Someone fashioned a cylindrical plug from a thick sherd and shaped it to fit the hole perfectly.

Some other medium-sized jars with handles apparently had deliberate holes in their sides, but the reason is completely unknown. The five hammerstones probably were used in groundstone manufacture, such as shaping metates, manos, donut stones, and other items. Also, when a mano and metate became smooth from use, they would be roughened by pecking them with a hammerstone. Household 1 did more manufacture of their groundstone tools than the other households, as evidenced by the high frequency of hammerstones. They may have made groundstone tools for exchange with other households.

The treatment of obsidian artifacts at the bodega is a microcosm of treatment within the site, so it is worth looking at in detail here. An obsidian blade in good, usable condition was kept in the roofing thatch only 20 centimeters from the north wall. As the roof peaks in the center and slopes down toward the edges, it would be more reachable than if it were stored toward the center of the thatch roof. It had been used, as some wear in the form of small nicks can be seen along both edges, particularly when examined under a binocular microscope with more than 100 power magnification. Some organic residues were found along each edge, and they may be remains from the blade's last use. However, some organic residues were implanted on obsidian blades when the roofs burned, and we are working to develop criteria to distinguish the two. Another prismatic blade was discovered in roofing thatch just inside the doorway, about 30 centimeters from the south wall. It looks as if someone could walk into the bodega, take one step in and one step to the left, and reach up for the blade. This blade shows virtually no wear. Although it is relatively short (4.9 centimeters), it was in excellent condition. One other single blade was found in the bodega in an unusual position. It was found tucked into a little crack at the bottom of the west wall of the structure. It is at the end of the access corridor across the structure, so if one knew where to look, it would have been easy to find by entering the building, heading straight across, and reaching down to pull it out of the crack. This blade, of more typical length (six centimeters), had relatively extensive wear on one edge, and the other edge was essentially unused.

A cluster of four prismatic blades had been placed together, in a bundle up in the roof in the center of the building. They would have been beyond the reach of anyone and would have required someone stepping up at least a meter high in the center to reach them. They probably were wrapped or tied together, as they survived the roof collapsing in a tight group. None of the blades show any evidence of use, even under 500 power magnification. Three of the four probably are from the same core, judging by their similarity in shape and technology as well as the visual characteristics of the obsidian. However, none refits directly onto another, so they did not come off the same area of the core. The fourth is thinner and is of a darker and less striated obsidian. The four evidently are a highly valued cache of brand new obsidian blades that were kept in one of the most inaccessible locations of the household.

An obsidian scraper was found behind the northern post, barely down into the posthole, behind the large fired clay storage vessel (pot 14). This was well hidden and would have required moving at least two pots to reach behind the post. Such scrapers were possibly used for processing deer hide, but probably they were more often used in de-pulping the leaves of the agave cactus to liberate the long, tough fibers, which were twisted into twine or rope. Its working end as well as the edges show considerable use, and it is likely that it had been resharpened numerous times by percussion blows to remove small flakes. Another scraper was found in the roofing thatch 30 centimeters from the south wall, where it would be reachable by someone walking straight into the bodega and then turning left when they had almost reached the back wall. It had been used extensively and resharpened a number of times and is now only about half its originally estimated length. It was used harshly. A small portion of a macroblade was found on the floor, wedged between a broken metate and the southern wall of the bodega. It was highly used for harsh cutting and scraping tasks, leaving much wear along both edges.

Outside the structure were a few discarded obsidian blades. They had become so dull from use that they were thrown away, and they were so dull that they posed no threat to anyone walking or crawling over them. They generally are short, broken segments, shorter than 4 centimeters.

The pattern of hiding individual obsidian knives or scrapers in roofing thatch in accessible locations is found in many other buildings at Ceren, not just bodegas. Although it is not as common, it is not unusual to find other obsidian implements tucked into convenient hiding places. Keeping a cache of mint-condition knives in an inaccessible location is common. It is also common to find a few very worn fragments of blades discarded outside of buildings. Most blades, however, must have been discarded at greater distances from the structures, as relatively few have been found near the buildings.

Not only were parts of broken pottery often retained, broken metates were useful too. Broken pots and broken metates show rounding on the broken edges, indicating that they had been deliberately smoothed or had become rounded by use after breaking. Two broken metates were found on the floor, upside-down, where they served as potrests. Round bottomed pots need to be supported, and they were wedged in with other pots against walls, or had rocks and broken metates wedged against them to hold them up. Hammerstones were often used for potrests, but the most common item was a plain, smooth river cobble. One hammerstone was, for unknown reasons, kept up in the roofing materials, likely on top of a rafter, east of the mounted metate.

Area B is the zone in the center of the structure, as designated by Beaudry and Tucker (1989), and it is largely devoid of artifacts. It connected with the doorway to the east and forms an accessway into the storehouse. It did have the cache of new blades put way up into the roofing thatch, along with a sherd that was stored high. Only two artifacts were found on the floor in this area, an upside-down partial metate and a partial jar. The partial jar was a broken pot, and they had retained the lower portion, since it could still be useful.

Area C is the southwest corner of the building, and it was kept relatively free of artifacts. Unfortunately, a large lava bomb, about one-half meter across, crashed through the roof and landed on and into the floor in this area. It smashed up a large storage vessel so badly that we could not tell if it was in floor contact or had been suspended from the ceiling. Pieces of string found near the lava bomb could have been used for suspending the vessel, tying elements of the roof support, or both. Our poor project ceramicist has a tremendous jigsaw puzzle job to put the hundreds and hundreds of tiny sherds back together to reconstruct the pot. An obsidian scraper, mentioned above, had been kept in the roof thatch and had been dislodged when the bomb landed.

Area D is somewhat similar to Area A in that it was loaded with artifacts, some in the roof and some on the floor. It is not as large an area and it is located immediately to the left as one enters the building. A piece of carbonized wood with cut marks was found in this area, near the obsidian that was found in the roofing. Cutting wood for large flat boards was rare at Ceren, but cutting wood for smaller items, such as posts and beams, was common. Large boards are difficult to cut without steel tools, and when Ceren residents wanted an extensive flat wooden surface for a door or a shelf, they lashed together a series of straight poles.

Just inside the doorway, to the left on entering, were a number of items kept on the floor. These are the most accessible items of the bodega. They include a spindle whorl probably used to make cotton thread, stored with red pigment (probably hematite, i.e., iron oxide) mixed with mica in some kind of organic container. The mixture of red paint and mica gives a glittery red color that is similar to, but not as glittery as, specular hematite paint. Specular hematite is a more rare, and presumably more expensive, pigment that is loaded with glittering crystals of iron oxide. Mixing hematite and mica may be a "poor person's specular hematite" paint. More of the hematite and mica was found in the kitchen of Household 1 about five meters to the south. Next to it was a Copador polychrome melon-stripe bowl, a food serving vessel. It probably was in active daily use, being found immediately inside the bodega. Near it was a Guazapa scraped slip jar that may have held a liquid. Both of these vessels are further examples of pots that were partially broken yet remained in service, perhaps with some changes in their function. The fact that Household 1 retained more broken vessels than the other households may indicate that they were not quite so well off. Or it might indicate a "packrat" syndrome, a reluctance to throw anything away that could conceivably have a use in the future.

Past the polychrome serving bowl was a stack of four pots, kept fairly near the door. The bottom vessel is an incensario (incense burner) with a pedestal base and a long handle with a face on it for decoration. It probably was used in household religious observances. Resting in its bowl were three

Figure 4–5. Southern part of the bodega. The smaller hemispherical pot at the bottom is upside down, and the larger pot is on its side. The smaller pot was capping the larger one, but the eruption pushed them over. The two donut stones were stored in the roofing and fell into similar orientations early during the eruption, for reasons that are not known.

pots, two Guazapa scraped slip jars and a Cashal cream type bowl. It is possible that these three pots were also used in family rituals, but apart from their association with the incensario there is no other evidence of this. All of the pots evidently were empty at the time of the eruption.

Slightly farther into the bodega and along the south wall was a large Guazapa scraped slip storage jar that was capped by a smaller hemispherical jar (Figure 4–5). The storage jar was tipped over to the south by the lateral force of the eruption, and the smaller jar capping it was pushed off of it, ending up to the south of the south wall. The displacement evidently occurred during the arrival of Unit 3. Neither vessel had any discernable contents before the eruption. The larger vessel's round bottom was stabilized by a number of means. It was resting against the south wall, and it had four things wedged up against it: a broken metate, a laja (a flat slab of andesite rock), a wedge of clay, and a stream rock. Why so much effort was expended to brace the vessel with five points of contact, in addition to the floor, is unclear. Had it held a liquid, that would have affected aeolian sedimentation inside the partially turned-over pot, but no evidence of that was encountered. It almost certainly was empty.

Just beyond the two vessels were a hammerstone, a pumice smoothing stone, and a duck. The duck, probably alive immediately before the eruption, was evidently tied to the south wall by a thin cord and probably

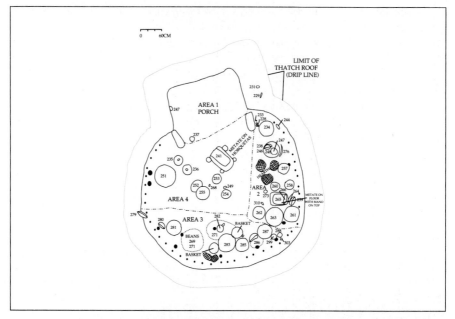

Figure 4–6. The kitchen of Household 1, known as Structure 11. The porch area was kept clean of artifacts; some artifacts were stored in the thatch roof. Area 4 was for food grinding and storage of cooking and other pots. Area 2 was the active food grinding, soaking, and cooking zone. Area 3 was for storage of food and implements.

was being kept for food rather than being the family pet. It died early in the eruption, probably during Unit 1 deposition. The very open walls of Structure 6 provided very little protection from the nasty tephra clouds coming in from the north.

Three donut stones were found in this area of the bodega. One was on the floor toward the back of Area D. There was no evidence of a pole or anything inside it. Two other donut stones were stored above the doorway and almost a meter inside, up with roofing supports. They tumbled down when Unit 1 was being deposited (Figure 4–5). The curious thing is that both were tipped in the same direction with the holes pointed toward the southeast. That might make sense if they were mounted on sticks, like the one leaning against the wall of Structure 1, but there was no evidence of sticks. Why, after falling from the rafters, they would be tilted in the same direction remains a mystery. Perhaps it was nothing but coincidence, or perhaps they had short sticks (pestles?) in them.

THE KITCHEN (STRUCTURE 11)

We first suspected there was a structure under volcanic ash when we noticed that the tephra layers were bulging a little, to the east of Structure 6. Two test pits were excavated through the rising tephra layers, and the presence of a structure was confirmed.

Structure 11 was the kitchen for Household 1. We had been looking for a kitchen for years. In the excavations of 1978 and 1989 we had yet to find a single cooking vessel with smoke incrusted on its bottom. It was an ample and well-organized kitchen, with some features not seen in other buildings excavated to date at the Ceren site. It is unusual in that it is circular, with very little bajareque and no solid adobe columns, and it was built on a very shallow platform. The floor was only five to ten centimeters above the surrounding ground surface, and the interior floor was not of fired adobe, as in the other structures, but of volcanic ash from the Ilopango eruption. This would be a very practical floor, as spills would seep into the floor. But when the floor became too organic-laden and dirty, it was easily replaceable. The edge of the floor, following the line of postholes, was 15 to 20 centimeters above the surrounding terrain, forming a barrier to moisture during heavy rains. With a diameter of four and a half meters and a small, rectangular porch, it had about 20 square meters of roofed internal space. The building is also unusual in that it opens directly to the north, in contrast to most building orientations. Its porch of fired adobe conveniently opens directly toward Structure 1 and the entry to Structure 6, the bodega. They form two edges of an open plaza.

The roof was supported by a series of 44 thin poles running around the circumference, by two large poles in the north end of the porch, and by two large poles running up from the bajareque "columns" at the entrance (Figure 4–7). The bajareque "columns" are 1.3 meters tall, a relatively short height for bajareque at Ceren. They are the remnants of a more extensive bajareque wall that largely had been removed; it may have encircled the

Figure 4–7. The kitchen, with the porch at the top, past the two bajareque columns. This area is now in the process of excavation.

entire kitchen. That wall was replaced by the vertical poles with vertical thatch supporting the thatch roof. This is the first thatch wall found at Ceren. A thatch wall would permit more air circulation but would permit more small creature circulation as well. The thatch roof was approximately a third the thickness of other thatch roofs excavated so far; this likely was to facilitate smoke leaving the structure. The roof collapsed earlier than that of any other building yet excavated at Ceren. It failed during the emplacement of Unit 1.

The early failure of the kitchen's roof had one beneficial aspect. It facilitated the preservation of painted gourds inside the structure. Usually when painted gourds decompose, the painted surface falls apart and only a few disassociated paint flecks are left for the archaeologist, at best. However, at the Ceren kitchen tephra filled in the inside and packed around the outside while the gourds still had strength. That gave us the opportunity to recover the gourds whole. It appears that Household 1 was using quite a few painted gourds in the kitchen, possibly in food preparation and probably in food serving.

The kitchen's south side, farthest from the entrance, had a shelf and a lot of artifacts. Two other postholes just inside the bajareque "columns" contained the horquetas that supported a metate at waist level. As with all the other metates associated with horquetas in Household 1, this metate showed very little use. A matching mano has yet to be found. All Household 1 metates may have been put on horquetas at about the same time, not very long before the eruption occurred. All are mounted relatively close to the ground, some 50 centimeters, and all have very slight use. If contemporary standards of mounting the metates, so the grinding surface is just below waist level, are applicable to the past, this indicates a short person was the principal food grinder in the family.

The southern end of the kitchen was used for storage. A shelf or long table was constructed at the southern end. Vertical posts supported a series of horizontal poles. Many artifacts were placed on top of the shelf, and some artifacts were stored on the floor under the shelf. Two large round-bottomed jars still were resting on their fiber rings that held them upright on the shelf. These fiber rings or donuts are the organic alternative to the potrests of stone and clay from the bodega, previously described. Also on the shelf were a celt (unhafted, like others at the site) and two small polychrome jars. Someone placed a red pigment with mica added, perhaps a "poor man's specular hematite," on the shelf. It may have been by itself, not in a container, as no sign of a container was found. This appears identical to the hematite-mica mixture found just inside the door of the bodega. A large jar was suspended above the shelf with a fiber rope, probably of agave.

Under the shelf were two baskets, an incensario, a large jar, and a small bowl. A miniature ceramic pot containing red pigment fell into the large jar, probably from the shelf above. Below the end of the shelf and resting on the floor was a surface of leaf matting which had a pile of beans placed on top of it. Three sizes or varieties of beans were being stored together. This is similar to bean storage at Structure 4, insofar as having an organic layer between adobe and the beans. The organic layer, in both cases, probably is to decrease capillary moisture from below. Two rodent skeletons were found, one near the beans and one with the shelf. Chiles were stored on the shelf or hanging from rafters. Other species tentatively identified in the field include achiote, cacao, and pumpkin. Not a single vessel from this area was soot-incrusted, indicating that they were not used in cooking.

The northwestern area was used for vessel storage. Two cooking vessels were stored there as well as some empty food storage and serving vessels. Two rodents were in the thatch above this area and one was on the floor.

The eastern side of the kitchen was the most actively used. East of the mounted metate was a well-used trough metate resting on the ground, stabilized by a rock, with its mano resting at the far, lower end. Both a large sherd and an open bowl were placed at the far end or lower end of the metate to catch the "masa." The masa is the mixture of ground maize and water. After it is ground, it is ready to be cooked. It is likely that they cooked tamales; no evidence of tortilla griddles has been found. Less than a half meter away was the three-stone hearth and a nearby pot with maize kernels soaking in it. The hearth had only a little charcoal in it and no pot on top. Cooking pots, with their smoke-blackened bottoms, were concentrated in this area. Cooking vessels were kept in the kitchen, and food was taken from the kitchen in serving vessels to the main structure for consumption. Cooking vessels are not found outside the kitchen. This area gives the appearance of being cleaned up for the night, rather than in active use during the day. The thatch roof was used to store an obsidian prismatic blade with an excellent cutting edge and five red pigment lumps. It is consistent with the storage of other knives in active use that this blade was stored immediately inside the doorway, to the left upon entering, up in the thatch.

The center of the room was kept relatively clear of artifacts. The porch entryway and the clear center of the structure give access to the three functionally different kitchen areas. One, the east side used for food processing, was described previously. The porch surface was kept clean, but the roof was used for storing an obsidian scraper, a deer-sized mammal longbone, and a bone tool. As with obsidian tool storage elsewhere, the obsidian scraper in frequent use was kept easily available by being up in the thatch roof past the east edge of the porch.

Many hemispherical painted gourds were found in the structure. Many of the gourds were painted red all over, while others were painted green, yellow, and other colors. That their greatest concentration in the site to date is in this kitchen, with a possible pile of nested gourds in the niche in Structure 2, indicates a function as food ladles and probably as food serving vessels for individuals. They probably used the large polychrome pottery bowls to serve the main course and the smaller gourds to serve other components of the meals.

Based on ethnographic analogy in the gender division of labor, Structure 11 probably was a female activity area focusing on food processing. A probable male activity structure for daytime activities evidently was Structure 5 (see next section, below), on the other side of the domicile. The kitchen was constructed with practicality in mind, and it was internally well-organized. It was amply stocked with cooking, storage, and food processing vessels and implements. And, those implements often went beyond the minimal requirements for function, as decoration of them was common and sometimes quite elaborate.

THE WORKSHOP (STRUCTURE 5)

A ramada structure, a platform with a roof but without walls, was located about 3.5 meters west of Structure 1. It was cut away by the bulldozer in 1976, leaving only its southern end. It was connected with Structure 1 with a walkway of stones. Its floor was kept clean of artifacts, and no artifacts were stored up in its thatch roof. Its function was divulged by the density of obsidian wastage from tool manufacture found to the south. It apparently was the workshop for making and resharpening obsidian tools. Ethnographically (looking for similar procedures in comparable living societies), chipped stone tool manufacture is a male activity, so this seems to be the men's workshop for daytime activities.

In overview, Household 1 had an astounding number of ceramic vessels. They had a total of 74 vessels that we excavated, including damaged but still serviceable vessels, but excluding the large sherds that they saved and used. Of that total, 28 came from the bodega, 15 from the domicile, 5 from the area under the eaves of the domicile, and 26 from the kitchen. Full excavation of the entire area of Household 1 could increase that by a dozen or more. And, as far as we can tell so far, Household 1 was the most humble found at the site to date. Given the variety of ceramic vessels, the volume of storage, the variety of grains stored, and the amount and quality of roofed space, I would judge the quality of life to be quite good 1400 years ago at Ceren. Unfortunately, the quality of life in the town today, by these same standards, is inferior.

ACTIVITY AREAS BETWEEN STRUCTURES

There are basically four types of spaces at Ceren, under roofs and inside walls, under roofs outside of walls, open areas, and cultivated areas. The amount of space outside the walls and under the eaves of most structures exceeds the amount of roofed space inside the walls. In this section we look at the spaces under the eaves and at the open areas, beginning with Structure 5 and moving east and south in Operation 1.

Most of the area around Structure 5 was kept clean of artifacts and features, with two exceptions. An area of obsidian wastage, of used up tools and resharpening debris, had accumulated to the south of the structure. A walkway was constructed from the structure to the main domicile, Structure 1, of stones and flat pieces of tuff. Tuff is a semi-consolidated volcanic ash from an eruption prior to Ilopango, and it makes a good material for a walkway. A thin scatter of sherds and charcoal was found along the walkway.

The area around Structure 1, under the eaves, was kept clean of artifacts for about three-quarters of a meter. It was built up as a raised walkway along the south side of the structure, indicating that the surface received a lot of traffic. However, the eaves past the southern corner of the structure were packed with artifacts, with some artifacts on the ground surface. Into the ground were mounted the two forked sticks, the horquetas, to support a metate. Its mano has not been found. This is a convenient grinding area just outside the domicile, close to the entrance to the bodega, and about seven meters from the kitchen. Stored above the metate in the roof were a figurine head and a polychrome bowl. On the ground surface were a few discarded sherds and a metate fragment. Just south of the mounted metate and up in the roofing supports were five pottery vessels. Two were polychrome bowls, two were globular jars, and one was the lower part of a jar. One of the polychrome pots was partially broken and had changed function into a pigment container. Beyond the clear, raised walkway was the original ground surface with occasional discarded sherds pressed into it. All had rounded edges, in contrast to the fresh breaks on sherds that broke from pots during the eruption.

The zones under the roof of Structure 6, outside all four walls extending 60 to 70 centimeters away from the walls, were kept clean of artifacts. Thus, the eaves of Structure 6 provided covered walkways. Perhaps it is not surprising that it would do so, as it is located toward the center of the Household 1 compound. The time frozen by the eruption apparently was the middle of rainy season (probably August), and it is likely that there was less foot traffic on these covered walkways during the dry season. It is also probable that some activities moved outside of the structures during the dry season.

Although some of the area between Structures 6 and 11 could not be excavated, enough was excavated to indicate that it was an area kept clear. The surface was kept clean of broken artifacts, and it was highly compacted. It appears to have been an area of considerable use. It is likely that, as food was being removed from storage, ground, processed, and cooked in Structures 6 and 11, many family members played and conversed in the open patio area.

Yet another structure was discovered during the 1990 field season a few meters east of Structure 6. It was given the name Structure 10 but has not been excavated; only the tops of some walls and a column have been found. It is of bajareque with adobe columns at the corners and probably measures some three by four meters. It caused a considerable bulge in the tephra layers as high as Unit 10, indicating that it probably has a high platform and that many of the walls withstood the vicissitudes of the eruptive phases. It is not known if it functioned as a part of the Household 1 com-

Figure 4–8. Maizefield excavated south of the kitchen. Ridges had clusters of 2 to 5 corn plants growing on top, spaced about every 60 centimeters, where small markers can be seen. The lowermost tephra layer is Unit 1, and the coarse layer above it is Unit 2 that fell very hot. Unit 3 is the thick, fine-grained layer at the top of the photograph.

plex or if it was separate from that household. In any event, it probably marks the eastern edge of the patio east of Structure 6.

THE GARDEN

A two by four meter area was excavated to the south of Structure 6, to explore the area between the bodega and the cornfield. A garden was found, organized into two neat rows paralleling the side of the bodega. The garden began only a few centimeters beyond the edge of the bodega's thatch roof. The rows follow the overall orientation of the site, 30 degrees south of magnetic east. Each row is about a meter apart, and the plants are spaced about 75 centimeters apart, leaving little doubt that they were planted deliberately. Clearly there were three species of plants, two of which were field identified (pending confirmation) as "macoyas" and bromilacea plants. The base of each plant had a small mound of soil packed up around it. This was a well-tended garden. We found the plants preserved as hollow spaces in the Units 1 and 3 tephra. The volcanic ash packed around the plants, and then the plants decomposed, leaving a hollow cavity. Unfortunately, the Unit 2 tephra does not preserve the cavities, so when the dental plaster is poured into the cavities from the Unit 3 tephra, it often "bleeds" into the Unit 2 coarse tephra.

THE MILPA (MAIZEFIELD)

Zier (1983) describes the two test pits excavated on the south side of the Household 1 area in 1978. One found a series of ridges, approximately following the overarching alignment of the site's architecture, with juvenile maize plants that had sprouted from the tops of the ridges (Figure 4–8). The field apparently is not irrigated, so the juvenile maize—probably a second planting—was obtaining moisture from the rain. The plants had grown to about 20 to 40 centimeters high, indicating the most likely month for the eruption is August. (One of the ironies of archaeology is that we can date the eruption and entombment of Ceren to the month, and perhaps to daytime or nighttime, but our best dating to the year is from radiocarbon dating, AD 590 plus or minus 90, which means there is a two-thirds probability that the true date lies within this range.) The diameters of the juvenile maize plants range from .6 to 1.3 centimeters. The maize plants are about one-half meter apart along the ridges, and the ridge tops are about .6 meters apart. Subsequent work around this test pit has indicated that multiple seeds were planted, and multiple maize plants had sprouted per location, with four being the most common (Murphy 1989). That is a pattern still practiced in many areas of Central America.

The other test pit (#1) excavated in 1978 (Zier 1983) encountered a maizefield that had been fallow or recently harvested before the eruption. The maize had been planted in ridges, like in the other test pit, but the ridge tops had been trampled. Some hazy footprints could be seen, and the successional grasses that had recolonized the fallow field were preserved as rust-colored plant impressions in the lowermost one to three centimeters of volcanic ash. The field had parallel ridges, also following the overall orientation of the site, but the parallel ridges were blocked by perpendicular ridges. Thus, these are blocking ridges, probably designed to maximize infiltration of water and minimize erosion. The young soil, formed on top of the volcanic ash from the Ilopango eruption a few centuries earlier, had suffered some erosion from cultivation by earlier Ceren residents, and evidently they had learned how to control, or at least minimize, erosion. If this interpretation is correct, this is rather sophisticated microtopographic slope management. The soil, analyzed by Olson (1983), indicated that it had minimal organic content, a pH of 7.1, was good in nitrogen and iron, but was weak in phosphorous, potassium, magnesium, calcium, and manganese.

SUMMARY

Household 1 was agrarian and craft-oriented. The residents had a garden nearby where they grew a variety of plants including manioc, and they grew maize farther out. It is likely that the men had to walk a considerable distance to their outer fields. The women made cotton garments, made agave fiber rope and twine, and scraped-slip utility storage and cooking vessels. They made their own grinding stones, including metates, manos, and donut stones. They used hematite, sometimes with mica added, to decorate things, probably including themselves. The household lived in a complex of buildings, each specialized to various tasks. One building was a storehouse, one was a male workshop, one was the kitchen, and one functioned as the living room, dining room, and bedroom. The family lived well, based on the ampleness of the architecture, the number and variety of the pottery vessels, the stored foods, and the range of stone and perishable artifacts. Their strong roofs of palm and grass thatch protected the buildings and their residents from the rain. But they did not protect them from the sudden eruption of what is now known as Laguna Caldera Volcano, particularly the second and third components of the eruption.

5

Household 2

☐

INTRODUCTION

Household 2 is not quite as thoroughly excavated as Household 1, but we do know quite a lot about it, certainly enough for a relatively detailed treatment here. Both the domicile and the bodega have been excavated, as well as some surrounding ground surface (Figure 5–1). Also, an enigmatic large structure was excavated to the south (Structure 9), as was a sizeable extent of maize milpa. There are some strong similarities in domiciles and bodegas between the two households, which tell us something about the culture. There are some interesting differences as well, which provide inklings about household specialization in a complex economic and social matrix.

Brian McKee has been in charge of the excavations in Operation 2, and his reports (1989, 1990) and an article (Sheets et al. 1990) are used as the basic material for this chapter.

STRUCTURE 2, THE DOMICILE

This structure was first suspected to be a prehistoric construction when geophysical anomalies were detected at this location. In 1979 and 1980 we detected an M-shaped anomaly in the resistivity data (Figure 3–4), and the radar data generated in 1979 also contained an intriguing anomaly at this location. The radar showed a strong reflector, now known to be the house floor, with bowed up tephra layers on top. That is from the raw radar data; I am afraid that if we digitize and mathematically caress the data we will have such detail that we may not have to excavate! The resistivity and radar anomalies were strong and both were in the same location, so we investigated further. The core drill rig borrowed from the *Centro de Estudios Geotecnicos* was put to use pulling up stratigraphic samples. This was the real test to see if the geophysical instruments really could detect buried structures. We photographed, measured, and described each, to keep track

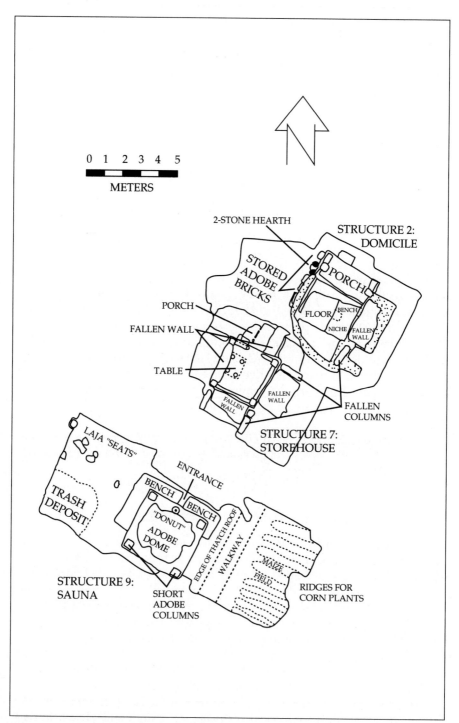

Figure 5–1. Map of Operation 2.

Figure 5–2. An architect's reconstruction of the domicile for Household 2 (Structure 2) and the bodega (Structure 7) behind it.

of each layer. Any deviation from the natural stratigraphic sequence could be an indication of human cultural activity, or it could be due to natural processes such as erosion or redeposition, and it was essential that we be able to tell the difference.

I decided to turn to geophysics, with desperation and a little bit of hope. This choice was about to be tested. My anxiety was fed also by the fact that I had convinced the National Geographic Society, Committee on Research and Exploration, that geophysical instruments might be able to detect buried structures as anomalies. The proposal was clearly written that it was a risk and that it might not work. However, it certainly would not help my credibility—if I went back to them in the future—if it all failed. Down deep, I had to admit that we had less than a 50/50 chance, but it was worth the try. Unknown to me, Bill Loker, my wonderful graduate student assistant, had smuggled a bottle of champagne out into the field every day of the 1980 field season, in case it worked. And it did! We celebrated for a long time, even going into town. A deep sample, from about five meters down, pulled up a sample that had the Preclassic clay soil made into a building floor, with a thin wisp of thatch roofing on top of the prepared clay surface! This "inverted stratigraphy" means that people took the clay that occurs naturally under the Ilopango ash and moved it on top of the ash, while constructing a dwelling. Although we did not know it at the time, the drill was perfectly situated. It pulled up a sample of the sub-platform mound to the southwest of the structure, so the drill bit did not affect any of the structure itself. I also had a nagging fear that it might work too well, and we might pull up part of a polychrome vessel or part of someone's cranium. We have calculated that the odds of this happening are very low, but they are real. We are now able to do less drilling, because we know where principal structure groups are located.

We considered using a bulldozer to remove the sterile (no artifacts) volcanic overburden from above and around Structure 2, since doing that by hand would be a long and arduous process. Many tons of ash needed to be hauled. Unfortunately, even a small bulldozer weighs a lot, and the vibration or compression can be destructive if a bulldozer gets too close to a prehistoric structure. Thus, we would have to leave more than a meter and a half of volcanic ash above all structures. That would mean many extra weeks of removal of volcanic ash by hand. We enlisted the assistance of a heavy equipment firm in San Salvador, and they suggested a large power shovel. That was ideal for our purposes because the weight and vibration of the machine are well to the side of where the bucket is doing the excavations. The bucket can lift almost a cubic meter, and it takes less than a minute to fill the bucket and empty it into a dumptruck. The shovel would fill the dumptruck in just a few minutes, but we soon ran out of places to put all that ash. We developed the "hauling ash" project, by spreading the word that we were making volcanic ash from the site available to anyone at no cost. By that time the site had developed a local mystique, so people really wanted it to level their patios and improve roads, and the school used it to level their soccer field. In fact, the "hauling ash" project was so successful that people wanting it would show up outside the site before dawn to be first in line.

Structure 2 is very similar to Structure 1, which should not be too surprising, as both are the domiciles for their respective households. The construction processes were similar, beginning with an irregular mound of clay that presently extends beyond the platform in all directions, evidently for drainage purposes. The platform, oriented 30 degrees east of magnetic north, is larger than Structure 1. It is 4.33 meters long, 3.4 meters wide, and three-quarters of a meter high. The platform and exposed surfaces of the substructure mound were fired before the walls and roof were built. The four solid adobe columns are so similar in size that we suspect a mold was used for their construction. The walls of the front porch have a feature not seen in other excavated structures—two solid adobe slab wing walls. Each measures 35 by 65 by 105 centimeters.

The doorway from the porch into the inner room passes through the bajareque partition wall. The top of the doorway is an adobe lintel supported by internal poles. It is 55 centimeters wide and one and a half meters high, very similar to most doorways at Ceren. Why doorways are so low, and consistently low, is unclear. Certainly most people would have had to duck while going through the doorways, since they are only five feet high. The sides of the doorway were enlarged or reinforced, creating a pilaster effect, and a cornice ran along the top of the entire wall. The mudded bajareque walls were 1.75 meters high above the floor, or 2.40 meters above the surrounding ground surface, sufficient to provide privacy in the inner room. Just inside the partition wall, and parallel to it, was a high shelf that ran the width of the building and extended beyond the walls to take advantage of the eaves. It was made of horizontal poles. Curiously, the parts extending beyond the walls, under the eaves, received special treatment. They were covered with grass and then a thick layer of wet mud. When that dried, it made a very hard overlying shelf well above the outside walkway that was not very accessible. That almost certainly was the objective.

As with Structure 1, the southern corner of the inner back room had a large adobe bench, filling almost one-half of the room. The Structure 2 bench was bigger than the Structure 1 bench, measuring 55 centimeters in height, and was about 1.5 by 2.5 meters in width and length. Its most interesting feature was the niche that was built into it when it was constructed (Figure 5–3). It is an opening about one-half meter cubed supported on horizontal rods of wood that were mudded over. The niche contained three polychrome vessels, all evidently involved in food serving. One is a Gualpopa open bowl with a slightly flattened bottom. Another is a Copador tripod bowl. It was upright in the niche, covered by a Copador Polychrome bowl (Figure 5–4) with melon stripe decorations, that was upside down. When this bowl was removed from the niche and cleaned carefully with brushes, the finger swipes of the person who ate from it 1400 years ago became visible (Figure 5–5). Because forks were invented in Italy only three centuries ago, people used to eat with their fingers, and we found the direct evidence of that. In fact, traditional households in Central America today use their fingers when eating much more than utensils.

It is fortunate that we learned years ago not to follow the usual archaeological procedures in artifact processing. At most archaeological sites the archaeologist, after mapping, describing, and photographing an artifact in its original location, lifts the artifact and sends it to the pottery lab. There someone carefully and thoroughly washes the pottery, and after it is dried and catalogued, the ceramic specialist analyzes it. That would have eliminated the finger swipes. We have learned to gently clean all artifacts with fine brushes before considering washing them with water. The Ceren polychrome serving bowl is on display at the Museo Nacional in El Salvador, having not been washed and with finger swipes visible.

The other important item in the niche was what we initially thought was a codex. A codex is a fan-fold document that is like a book. It can record religious matters or more mundane items. Based on deer hide or amate bark paper, both sides of codices were painted and then folded in on themselves multiple times. Archaeologists have, upon occasion, come across places in Maya sites where they thought a codex had been, but they found only some isolated paint flecks, and no painted surface was reconstructible. The area of the niche with the painted item seemed to be in better condition than those finds of paint flecks, so we decided to try to recover the item by a procedure called "block lifting." The painted area was careful-

Figure 5–3. The niche in the bench, immediately after it was uncovered. Two pots are right-side up, and one is upside down. To the left is the painted artifact; at first it was thought to be a codex, but now we think it may have been a set of nested polychrome painted gourds.

Figure 5–4. The pot that was upside down in the niche, after cleaning. A band of human faces adorn the top, with broad melon stripe decoration on the bottom.

ly isolated, and then the item, along with a section of the adobe floor of the niche, was lifted all together as a block. That evening I called a number of archaeologists, from Los Angeles to Washington D. C., to get advice on how to handle such an item and to determine who would be the best person to help. Many people agreed that the best person in the U.S. is Harriet "Rae" Beaubien of the Conservation Analytical Laboratory, Smithsonian Institution. She was able to treat the fragile artifact in El Salvador and then take it to her laboratory. She has determined that the sides of the organic layer were painted white with kaolinite (a pure clay) and then painted with cinnabar (mercuric sulfide, a strong red color), limonite (an iron oxide), a green pigment with serpentine, and other pigments.

We had thought that it most likely was a codex until we found a series of painted gourds, many painted with similar designs to that on the niche artifact in the kitchen of Household 1 (see preceding chapter). Now we feel that the niche object more likely was a set of nested painted gourds on which the painted surfaces collapsed onto the flat surface of the niche floor when the gourds themselves decomposed. The gourds probably were used for food serving. It is possible that they were used to ladle food from larger vessels, and they could well be individual serving vessels. The fact that mercury is toxic if ingested in significant quantities becomes important. Mercuric sulfide is one of the most highly toxic forms of mercury. In the future, when we find human bone, we will determine if there are significant amounts of mercury showing up in the bone. There are potential health implications to using a mercuric-based pigment on a food vessel, and it will be interesting to see how successful they were in avoiding those problems.

An enigmatic item was suspended from the ceiling in Structure 2. Not only do we not know what it was doing there, but we are puzzled by having found it in some other structures we have excavated at the site (Structures 2, 3, and 4). In all cases it was suspended in the center of the building, probably in an organic container, but we have yet to find definite evidence of the nature of the container. It is a large (approximately 30 to 50 centimeters in diameter) mass of Ilopango volcanic ash mixed with water and short pieces of grass. It was mixed vigorously enough to have included bubbles in it, and kept moist. It might have been a cleanser, like Ajax but without the soap, to clean food vessels, floors, walls, and the like. We do not know.

No artifacts were found on the bench, but a number of artifacts were found on top of a thin dusting of Unit 1 that had blown onto the bench before they fell. That indicates that they had been stored above the bench, likely on the long shelf that ran above it. Three ceramic vessels were stored there, a globular scraped slip jar, a smaller scraped slip jar, and an incensario that likely was used in family ritual. The bench was kept clear for family use.

The floor and roof of the south (inner) room were also kept quite clean, more clean than the analogous inner room of Structure 1. That contrasts with the north room, where a lot of obsidian was stored up high. Two prismatic blades (Figure 5–6) were kept in the north room thatch, in accessible locations near the doorway. One was complete and barely used. The

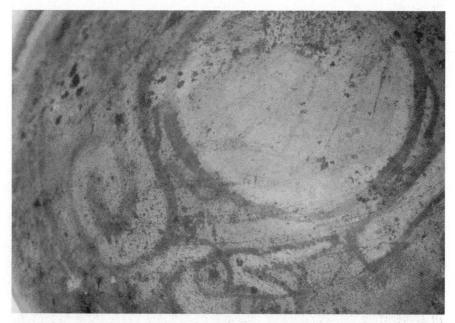

Figure 5–5. The inside of the pot was also polychrome painted. This type of vessel has been thought by archaeologists to have been used as a food-serving vessel. With the excavation of this pot, there is no doubt about it, as the finger swipes of food can still be seen.

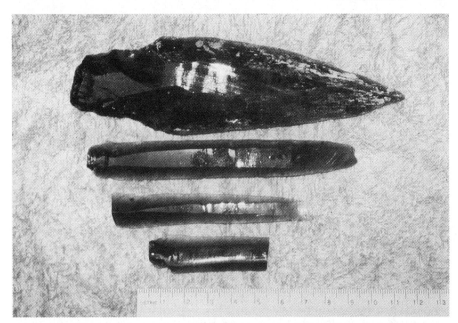

Figure 5–6. Four obsidian artifacts that were stored in the roof thatch of Structure 2.
At the top is a stemmed macroblade apparently used, hand-held, as a knife. The others are
prismatic blades; the longest is complete and the other two are partial blades. They remain
extremely sharp.

other blade was broken and had moderate wear along with some organic residues. A large stemmed macroblade was also kept in the roofing and was in very good condition. It is a visually impressive artifact that uses up a lot of obsidian and, therefore, had a high intrinsic value. It is possible that it was used as a large knife for cutting tougher materials than those that can be cut with the more fragile primatic blades. One edge was more used than the other. The stemmed portion may have been shaped to hold onto it by hand, as there is no evidence that it was hafted to a handle. A small side scraper was found on top of Column D, with no use wear visible. It apparently had been resharpened just before the eruption.

The north room also had a Cashal cream storage vessel stored up in the roofing. The only artifact that was in direct floor contact was a series of small poles that were lashed together with string. We found 31 holes and cast them with dental plaster. It apparently was a movable fence feature of some sort. A very similar one was found on the floor by the front door of the Household 2 storehouse (Structure 7). Two lashed pole fences were found under the eaves of Structure 4 and under a storehouse as well, but their functions in any of these structures are unknown.

We found some interesting things to the southwest of the structure, just outside the walls. They may have been stored on the relatively inaccessible shelf. Two donut stones were stored up high, under the eaves, and fell during Units 3 and 4 of the eruption. One had organic material caked on it and in the perforation, indicating that its interpretation as a club head, a scepter, or as a digging stick weight would be incorrect. It also had a small piece of a hardwood stick projecting out of it, and the perforation inside it had worn asymmetrically. All of these indicated that it was a perforated mortar. Evidently it was used to grind small amounts of food, perhaps nuts, with the ground portion falling through the perforation. A few meters beyond the edge of the roof was a trash area with discarded potsherds. With them were found a tooth of a carnivore, probably a domesticated dog, and a freshwater snail locally called a "jute." As mentioned in Chapter 3, this indicates that the nearby river was clean, in unfortunate contrast with contemporary conditions.

The area west of the structure was used for storage under the eaves and for a small hearth. The hearth was a surprise, as it was immediately against the platform of the structure. In fact, the platform edge provided the third point of support, as there were only two stones of the usual three-stone hearth. There was some charcoal accumulation at the bottom and some oxidation of the surface below the fire and along the vertical surface of the platform, but both charcoal and oxidation were minimal, indicating very little use. People must have watched this fire carefully, knowing that if it got out of control, it could easily catch the thatch roof on fire. No vessel was found on top of the hearth, as with the hearth in the kitchen of Household 1. The hearth was built in an area that was used to store adobe bricks. The sun-dried adobe bricks were of two sizes, one about 55 centimeters long and the other about 95 centimeters long. One curious aspect of this is that we have yet to find adobe bricks used in construction at the Ceren site, yet they were storing them under the eaves, out of the rain. Adobe brick construction is known from the site of San Andres, the major site dominating the valley at the time.

A medium-sized donut stone was stored high, above the adobe bricks, but fell early in Unit 3 deposition and broke when it landed. It was stored near a fine sandstone whetstone which similarly was dislodged and fell under the eaves. These artifacts probably were stored up on the relatively inaccessible shelf, indicating that their owner was trying to keep them away from casual manipulation. Sandstone does not occur naturally in this volcanic area, so this stone probably had to be carried in from the north about 50 kilometers. It likely was used to sharpen groundstone implements such as celts. The shapes of the ground areas match the shapes of celt bits.

In general, the domicile of Household 2 was somewhat larger and better constructed than the domicile of Household 1. It also had floors that were kept more clear of artifacts, and it had fewer craft areas.

STRUCTURE 7, THE BODEGA

Structure 7 (Figure 5–7) is the bodega for Household 2. The domicile, Structure 2, is only 1.2 meters to the northeast, and their thatch roofs almost touched each other. Structure 8 is located a short distance east of Structure 7 and might be the kitchen for the household. It has not yet been

excavated; only a small bit of architecture and one artifact have been excavated so far. If it is the kitchen, it probably is of more substantial construction than the kitchen of Household 1.

The architecture of Structure 7 is described here in order of construction. First, a sizeable clay mound was constructed, probably for
drainage of rain water away from the building. For some reason, the subplatform mound of Structure 7 extended more than a meter from the platform walls. At least on the north side this provided ample roofed
household activity area and was used for eating maize on the cob just
before the eruption struck. A square platform of solid adobe was constructed that was slightly over three by three meters and was built about a meter
above the surrounding terrain. This is considerably more substantial than
Structure 6.

A large porch about three and a half square meters was added to the
north side. The exposed portions of the mound, the platform, and the porch
were fired, perhaps before the adobe columns were mounted in the corners.
The columns are about 1.55 meters high, and most bajareque walls are
about the same height. The vertical poles in the bajareque walls penetrated
well into the platform, probably to supply strength to the walls, in addition
to their being anchored above with the roof.

The northern bajareque wall, with the entrance doorway, was
emphasized over the others and measures 1.67 meters in height. This is similar to, but not nearly as extreme as, the emphasis of the Household 1 bodega entrance wall (Structure 6). Handles salvaged from broken pottery
vessels were mounted inside the doorway wall to secure the front door. The
front door was made of vertical poles lashed together with twine. The poles
rested on the lower surface of the porch, and some went into sockets of
small postholes to further secure the front door. Thus, the front door was
relatively substantial.

The vertical poles from the bajareque walls continued upward and
supported the roof, assisted by large posts set into and north of the porch.
Pieces of twine were the lashing connecting vertical and horizontal members of the roof. The excavated thatch was five to ten centimeters thick; the
degree of thinning due to the fire and the tephra overburden is unknown.
The thatch roof was extensive; in addition to covering the ten square meters
inside the walls, it covered some 27 square meters outside the walls. Only
in a few cases did thatch roofs cover more internal than external space at
Ceren; this structure is at the other extreme of the spectrum. The amount of
grass and palm used in re-thatching roofs at Ceren must have been tremendous. We do know that some palm trees grew in a line a few meters to the
west of Structure 7, as we found their hollow cavities in the volcanic ash,
and it is likely that they were used for thatch.

An unexplained, or at least not understood, feature is an adobe
"step" or small "bench" on the west side, abutting the platform. Its dimensions of 87 centimeters in length, 44 centimeters in width, and 34 centimeters in height would certainly make it a prime candidate for being a step,
but the west side is an unbroken bajareque wall. Hence, if it was a step, it

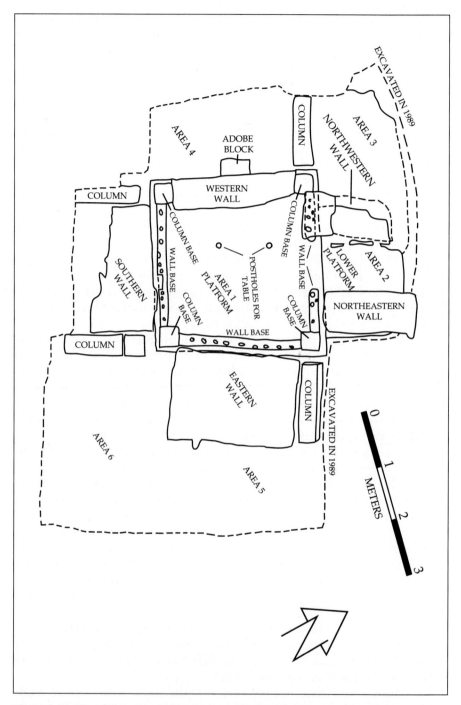

Figure 5–7. Map of Structure 7, the storehouse (bodega) for Household 2. All bajareque walls and all columns fell during the eruption when Unit 3 was being deposited. It was loaded with pottery vessels, the majority of which were being stored off the floor, suspended by ropes or on shelves. Area 3 is where the maizecobs were tossed after someone ate maize.

was in use when the entrance to the building was on the west side. It might have served as a small bench or seat along that side, under the eaves. Unfortunately we were not able to excavate along that side because the west wall fell into the building, and for conservation and display purposes the bottom part of that wall had to be left in place.

A wooden shelf or table was constructed on the western side of the room, supported by large wooden posts. It was at least a square meter and probably double that size. As in Structure 11, the shelf was made of horizontal poles that were lashed together. A rolled-up or folded-over mat was stored on its north end.

Structure 7 suffered more structural damage from the eruption than any other bajareque structure yet excavated, as all walls and all columns fell. Again, this structure anchors an end of the spectrum, as other structures with bajareque walls and adobe columns had at least some structural elements that stood throughout the eruption. (Structures 3 and 9, with solid adobe walls, suffered no wall collapses at all.) Unit 1 packed on the roof of Structure 7 and onto exposed surfaces, and a little blew into the building. Unit 2, with its clasts hotter than 575 degrees Celsius, set fire to the roof. Unit 3 continued to burden the roof until the combined effects of weakening by fire and overburdening by tephra resulted in collapse.

In bajareque buildings at Ceren the principal structural resistance to stress from wind, earthquake, and so forth, is in the interconnectedness of bajareque wall poles being tied to roofing members. Walls and columns were not structurally interconnected, but rather were only abutting, with their junctures smoothed over with clay surfacing. Therefore, the failure of the Structure 7 roof left the walls and columns vulnerable, and they all collapsed shortly after the roof fell.

The nature and density of internal artifacts indicate this was a bodega. A series of five large storage jars lined the back wall and were in direct floor contact. Most are Guazapa scraped-slip vessels. In addition to these, one medium-sized and two large pots were placed on the floor. They were storing various kinds of seeds.

A surprisingly large number of artifacts were suspended from the roof inside the bodega. (The majority of artifacts were stored in elevated contexts, above the floor.) The majority of ceramic vessels were suspended rather than on the floor. As archaeologists, we had no reason to suspect this from previously gathered data at other sites, and this requires attempts at explanation. A couple of practical reasons are (1) rodent and insect pests would have more trouble getting to something suspended from the ceiling than sitting on the floor, and (2) efficiency in utilization of space. If all of the artifacts we found stored with the roof were placed on the floor, the interior of this bodega would be too crowded to be very usable.

A cache of five miniature pottery vessels (Figure 5–8), seven jade beads, two other beads, and six shell fragments was found in Unit 3 in the southwest corner. They had been stored high in that back corner of the bodega in an organic container and fell with the roof. Most of the jade beads were biconically drilled, but two were cylindrically drilled, a relatively unusual way of perforating them. They are 1.4 to 1.7 centimeters in diameter. The other two beads were of shell and of a dense gray stone. A shell pendant, carved in the shape of a five-pointed star, was found nearby. It is possible the nine beads and the pendant were a necklace, but no string was found.

All five miniature pots contained red paint, and all were decorated. The pigment is mercuric sulfide (HgS), and it is so pure that some kind of refining may have occurred. The hues vary slightly and probably are deliberately different. One of the miniatures had a face on one side and a coiled tail on the other. The miniature pots are so identical at the mouth that they probably were made on a mold. I think the paint in them was liquid when the eruption struck, because of the flat surface it achieved after it fell in the pots, but Brian McKee thinks it could have been dry. We would like to know what things were being decorated with the cinnabar paint; the red color of the multilayered painted artifact from the niche in Structure 2, only a few meters away from these pots, is cinnabar. It is possible that the household engaged in painting gourds.

Nine other ceramic vessels or partial vessels were stored high inside the bodega, two probably on the shelf and the others connected with roofing. These include a polychrome tripod plate, a polychrome bowl with three monkeys, two medium-sized jars, and two dishes.

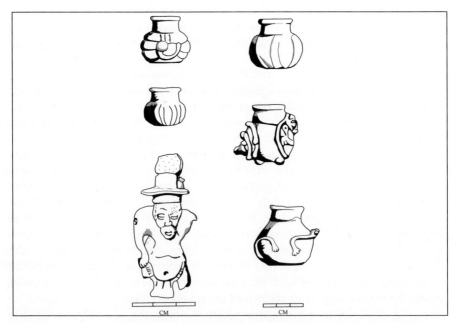

Figure 5–8. Miniature fired clay pots, used to store different hues of red paint made of cinnabar (mercuric sulfide). Each is uniquely decorated but of precisely the same size at the top. The tiny bone figurine was kept near the paint pots.

A greenstone celt was found inside one of the large storage vessels lining the south wall. It was in Unit 3 tephra inside the pot and had fallen into the pot during the third phase of the eruption. It was well made and highly polished at the bit end from manufacture and from use. There was no evidence of it having been hafted to a handle.

All obsidian implements were kept in the same area within the structure. Five prismatic blades were stored in roofing thatch at the southern edge of the structure. The thatch roof probably was too high toward the center of the structure to reach the thatch conveniently. Although some blades were snapped into shorter segments when the roof fell, their edges were in excellent condition prior to the eruption and remained in very good condition.

All roofs excavated so far at Ceren have small rodents, but bodegas are becoming known for having more than most. This bodega roof had five. As our Salvadoran workers noted, some things change with time, and some things do not. They have to take anti-rodent precautions today that are similar to their ancestors' at Ceren.

A carved bone figurine (Figure 5–8), in the form of a man with a hat, was found in very good condition. It was stored high, perhaps with roofing, and fell into a pot. Another important organic item is a nut shell perforated by a wooden stick, forming a spindle and spindle whorl. As with so many artifacts found at Ceren, this would not be preserved at most archaeological sites.

The porch had no floor contact artifacts, as it apparently was much used by household members, probably for varied tasks and activities. The adobe surfaces showed the effects of use; they were quite eroded. Although the surface was kept clean, there were quite a few elevated items, including a large sherd for storage of some unknown substance in the rafters, two polychrome bowls, sherds, a prismatic blade and a macroblade of obsidian, some paint, two deer bones, and a hemisphere of wood ash.

Lumps or hemispheres of wood ash are common in bodegas. Apparently the wood-ash remains of fires would be gathered up and placed in gourds and stored. The most likely use is in soaking maize kernels overnight prior to grinding them, as is still done in traditional households in Central America. The objective is to soften the shell of the kernel. In areas with limestone available, burned limestone is preferred, but wood ash is a viable substitute. It is not unusual for a bodega at Ceren to have a dozen hemispheres of wood ash.

Northwest of the structure were some sherds and obsidian blades that were discarded trash, a fragment of a bone needle, and some maize cobs. Although they sound mundane, the maize cobs were pretty exciting to encounter, as they really have that human touch. Someone had a taste for maize on the cob. Presumably, the maize on the cobs were boiled or roasted before eating, as mature maize that is uncooked is very tough. The maize cobs, now preserved by dental plaster, may have been tossed there by people eating while seated on the porch.

Immediately west of the structure, under the eaves and outside the walls, were two bowls, part of an obsidian macroblade, two manos, and two hemispheres of wood ash. All of these were stored high and fell when the roof collapsed early in Unit 3.

THE MILPA (MAIZEFIELD)

A milpa (maizefield) was found south of Structure 7 and east of Structure 9 (Figure 5–9). The agricultural field began one meter east of the eastern edge of the thatch roof of Structure 9. That provided a one-meter wide outside pathway between the roof edge and the field, and it was well-packed down. The maize plants were encountered as hollow cavities, preserved as casts by the Units 1 and 3 fine-grained base surge tephra units. The Unit 2 tephra, being largely airfall and coarse, unfortunately did not preserve the maize stalks. A total of eight ridges were excavated within the three by six meters of milpa exposed, but the milpa extends to the south, east, and north for unknown distances. The ridges are aligned to the overarching site alignment, 30 degrees south of east. The ridges themselves are 10 to 20 centimeters high and are about 80 centimeters apart. Usually there are multiple sproutings per planting location, with three to four plants being common, but the range is one to five. Most plant clusters, but not all, had small mounds of the *tierra blanca joven* tephra and soil built up around them, as was found in the Household 1 milpa (Zier 1983). Here, plant spacing is slightly greater than the Household 1 milpa. The striking difference is the youngness of the Household 1 milpa; it had been growing only for a few weeks. In contrast, this milpa had large mature plants with maize cobs that are 15 to 20 centimeters long. Either these plants began growing a couple of months earlier than the Household 1 milpa, or they are remnants from the previous year's growth. Most of the maize cobs were on stalks that were snapped over and left dangling, which is a method of drying and storing the maize still on the plant in the field. This technique of field storage is still used in the area today.

SUMMARY

Of the two domiciles excavated at Ceren so far, the domicile of Household 2 (Structure 2) was better constructed. It was kept more clear of artifacts. It had a niche in the bench that contained food serving vessels. One of the vessels had what archaeologists love to encounter, the "smoking gun" that indicates unequivocally the function of an item in a past society. The finger swipes in food remains in the polychrome bowl show, beyond a reasonable doubt, the function of that vessel. The family's cutting tools were neatly kept up in the thatch roof by the entrance to the structure, much as the Machiguenga in the Peruvian Amazon rainforest routinely stick their machetes up into the thatch roofs above the doorways to their houses when they enter (Allen Johnson, personal communication, 1990).

Figure 5–9. Three rows of maize plants found in the milpa south of Structure 7 and east of Structure 9. The maize plants are mature, and many have the stalks doubled over, with ears of maize still attached. This is a storage technique still used in Central America, for milpas close to the house. Multiple grains were planted per locality, and most localities had two to five plants that grew and matured. The ridges on which the planting was done can be seen continuing back into the unexcavated part of the milpa.

The Household 2 bodega was built on a much more substantial platform than that of Household 1, and the walls were much more solid and were anchored with adobe columns. Both bodegas were well stocked with ceramic storage vessels containing abundant seeds. The Household 2 bodega had a sizeable porch on its north side, and that may have been the place where people sat, ate maize on the cob, and threw it over to the west, just before the eruption struck. A temporary cache of valuables had been tucked in the back right corner of the bodega. It consisted of five miniature paint pots, beads of jade and other materials, a shell pendant, a bone figurine, and other items. Obsidian blades were kept in the thatch near the back wall of the bodega.

We have yet to excavate the kitchen of Household 1, and the residents might have had other specialized buildings like the workshop (Structure 5). At present it is not clear what the relationship was between the household and Structure 9. This building, described below, could have been a major source of wealth for the household, if it was affiliated with them. At any rate, Household 2 seems to have been more wealthy than Household 1, and less craft-oriented, judging by their architecture and personal possessions. However, the differences are not great.

6

Other Structures at Ceren

□

INTRODUCTION

In the previous two chapters we looked at the two households at Ceren where we have two or more buildings excavated and thus can get some idea about the activities within households. During the most recent season of fieldwork, during 1990, we found and excavated the bodega (storehouse) for yet another household, named Household 4. The building is formally designated Structure 4. We will look at it in considerable detail, as it is our first solid evidence of the next household to be excavated at Ceren. In the remainder of the chapter we will examine three other structures that do not fit into the suite of buildings that composed households. They are special buildings that were built to house specific activities, and they are understood to varying degrees. Each can be used as an example of the archaeological process of accumulating data, testing various interpretations, and coming up with the interpretation that best fits the data. One structure is a big community building, probably for neighborhood use, one is a strong adobe structure that evidently was a sauna, and one is a delicate and complex structure that may have belonged to a shaman.

STRUCTURE 4, THE BODEGA FOR HOUSEHOLD 4

Andrea Gerstle (1990) excavated the bodega (Structure 4) of Household 4 in 1990 (Figure 6–1). Although it is not necessary to present the amount of time it took to detect and excavate all structures, Structure 4 will be so documented as an example. It was first detected as a geophysical anomaly in 1979 and then checked again in 1980 and 1989, using resistivity and ground-penetrating radar (Loker 1983, Spetzler and Tucker 1989). Its excavation was delayed by complex land ownership negotiations, and it was decided that Structure 3, some 15 meters east, would be excavated first because it was more clearly owned by the Salvadoran government. Because of overpopulation of the country, land ownership is a very sensitive topic,

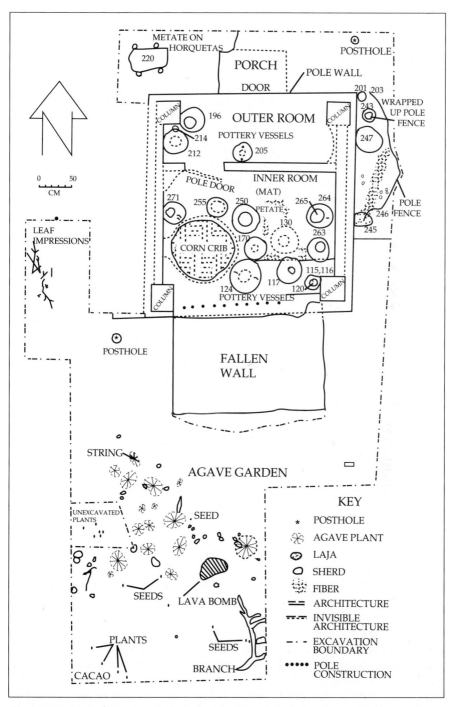

Figure 6–1. Map of Structure 4, the bodega for Household 4, showing architecture and artifacts.

and archaeologists must be very careful and respectful. Whenever we wish to walk a field in cultivation to check for prehistoric remains, we talk first with the landowner or the person leasing the land. Rarely do we have trouble obtaining permission to survey or excavate, once we make clear what we want to do and why.[6] We pay landowners for any damage done to crops, and we backfill excavated areas as a routine procedure.

At Ceren, our access complexities began in the late 1970s when El Salvador began some agrarian reforms that, at least in the early days of the program, really did benefit many rural farmers. The area that includes the Ceren site became a part of that program, and farmers were allowed to lease the land for a few years while they learned modern agricultural techniques. Eventually they could purchase the land at a reduced price and for the first time in their lives actually own land from which they could support their families.

A local peasant named Salvador Quintanilla began leasing Lot 189A, the present surface that is five meters above what we now know is the Ceren site. When we first came to the site, in 1978, he exhibited quite an interest in our findings. When we returned in 1979 with the radar, he was instrumental in obtaining an oxcart and two oxen, and he served as the oxcart driver. He has since become a close friend and trained archaeological worker. He also routinely takes people from San Salvador, the United Nations, the Organization of American States, and other organizations, on tours of the site. It has been immensely complex to find land of equal or greater value to substitute for his Lot 189A. Finally, a very fertile plot was found, and he is now the owner of it. Fortunately, he continues to be a valued worker when we are conducting field research, as his knowledge, experience, and enthusiasm for archaeology has grown. It was because of his changing ownership from one lot to the other, that we had to restructure our research program. We delayed the excavations of Structure 4 and accelerated the excavations of Structure 3.

Another building has been detected near Structure 4, just to the northwest. The edge of a subplatform was found in the northwest corner of the Operation 4 excavations, and many fragments of broken bajareque wall were found in Units 1 through 5 tephra layers in that area, probably blown in from the structure. Because the domicile (living-dining-sleeping) structures of Households 1 and 2 were located north of the bodega, it is possible that this is the domicile of Household 4, as it lies to the north of the bodega. Future excavations will determine its nature and function.

The excavations of Operation 4 began in mid-July and continued until mid-December of 1990. That the excavations took five months, with an excellent Salvadoran crew of eight, is indicative of conditions very different from the usual housemound in Mesoamerica. Had this bodega been abandoned in the usual fashion, with people taking away the usable vessels, food, and other items, and people still living in the area scavenging other items including architecture, there would have been very little remaining a year after they left. After that, the tropical sun and rains would cause further deterioration, aided by flora and fauna. An archaeologist, with the same size and training of a crew, would be able to excavate such a building in a week or two. That it took so long to excavate is indicative of preservation conditions at Ceren and to the limitations of normally abandoned structures. Excavations began with three two-by-two meter test pits which successfully located and determined the orientation of Structure 4.

A duralite roofing module was constructed above the area to protect the structure from rain, sun, dust, and wind. The duralite modules, each covering seven by seven meters, were our salvation. They were roofing a school in San Salvador, but the big 1986 earthquake destroyed the walls and the inside of the school. The roof largely survived and was salvaged. Later, international aid replaced the entire school, so the government donated 20 roof modules for our use. Architectural preservation of the site is so good that we have to erect protective roofing over all prehistoric structures before excavating them.

Early in the excavations, in the top layers of volcanic ash well above the Ceren site structures, a Postclassic midden (trash deposit) was found. It was buried in tephra layers from the Boqueron eruption, deposited well after the Laguna Caldera eruption (see Figs. 1–5 and 3–6). The midden is from people living in the area a few centuries after the Ceren site was occupied, and it is almost certain that they had no idea what lay a few meters below them. Boqueron, the main crater of San Salvador Volcano, erupted explosively sometime between AD 800 and 1200 and deposited a pasty wet blanket of volcanic ash over adjoining portions of the Zapotitan Valley. Although the Boqueron tephra was not intact over large areas of Operation 4 within the site, it was in situ in a few places. The artifacts apparently were from the soil developed on top of the tephra. A considerable amount of ceramics and obsidian was recovered. The obsidian was from a small workshop where they were making blades to serve as cutting implements.

By mid-August of 1990, three bajareque wall tops and four adobe column tops were uncovered. It was immediately clear that this bajareque structure was in better condition than most at the site. Most bajareque walls at Ceren were vulnerable to collapse after their roofs burned and collapsed, and most bajareque structures had many of their walls collapse. For example, all walls and all columns of Structure 7 collapsed. Only the south wall of Structure 4 collapsed, so the excellent architectural preservation provided an opportunity for conservation of walls prior to their being excavated. This may be a first in archaeology, doing architectural conservation of walls prior to excavating them. While the tephra layers were still in place on both sides of the walls, Victor Manuel Murcia and the architectural conservation team investigated each vertical hole where a vara (pole) had been placed in the wall. Most penetrated some 20 centimeters into the platform, and some went more than 30 centimeters. The hole where the rod had been was measured for diameter and length and a match in diameter, length, and species was obtained. The contemporary varas were gently slid down into the holes and solidified prior to continuing the excavations. The walls thus were reinforced by us in the same way they were reinforced by Ceren's original residents prior to the Laguna Caldera eruption, so they can now sustain wind stress and earthquakes. They would be very fragile without this reinforcement. It would be a crime to abruptly take these 1400-year-old structures into the present but give them a very short future by inadequate conservation.

Structure 4 probably was constructed over a substructure mound, but little of that mound was excavated for a variety of logistical reasons. The formal platform, built on top of the presumed mound, measures 3.2 by 3.25 meters, and averages 70 centimeters in height. The top surface slopes slightly down from the northeast corner, reflecting the slope of the general topography. The slope is so slight—just a few centimeters—that it is detectable only with instruments, and it is likely that the household members were unaware of it. The platform top and edges were resurfaced by a fine clay mixture, generally less than one centimeter in thickness. The entire platform was allowed to dry and then was fired, to create a massive fired brick block.

Four columns were mounted at the structure's corners, inset a few centimeters. Each column was 35 centimeters in length and width, and 1.4 to 1.45 meters in height. All tops were modified to support north-to-south horizontal roof beams; clay was packed around the beams to structurally affix them to the columns and likely to the varas exiting the bajareque walls. The beams run adjacent to, and inside of, the tops of the two bajareque walls. The beams were daubed with mud, forming a kind of internal rounded cornice. This extra reinforcement contributed to the building's strength and resistance to the buffeting from the eruption.

The bajareque walls are ten to 13 centimeters thick, with two centimeter diameter varas every 15 to 20 centimeters extending up above the clay-daubed portions of the walls, to assist in roof support. Only the south wall collapsed during the beginnings of Unit 3 emplacement. There is no evidence that it had additional reinforcement by a horizontal beam at the top. The internal dividing wall did have a horizontal beam at its top, and it survived the eruption's turbulence. The wall was perforated by a doorway 60 centimeters wide that is offset to the west. Clay was packed around the beam to form a squared cornice along the wall's north face. The effect is something like the upper cornice in the partition wall of Structure 2. Thus it appears clear that the additional reinforcement by a horizontal beam at the top of the mudded part of the bajareque wall made the difference. The walls that had it did not collapse, and the wall that did not have it collapsed when the roof failed.

The internal wall created two rooms (Figure 6–2), the north and the south. The north room is small, about one by 2.7 meters. Most of its artifacts were on a high shelf made of horizontal poles tied together with two-ply string. The shelf was surfaced with a thin layer of clay mixed with grass to create the top surface. The shelf evidently ran from the western to the eastern horizontal roof beam; one would have to duck under it and the wooden

Figure 6–2. Structure 4, largely excavated. The front (north) room is on the right, and the inner (south) room is on the left, with the circular maize crib visible. The walls have been consolidated with new rods to reinforce them. Two pots that fell from a high shelf can be seen at the far side of the front room. A metate just outside the structure, but under the eaves, can be seen at the upper right.

lintel of the doorway to enter the back room. The internal doorway had a wooden door consisting of two rows of vertical poles tied together in pairs with two-ply twine. When people wished to close off the inner south room, they must have tied the door to the vessel handles that were embedded into the south side of the doorjams. This door also was closed at the time of the eruption, as with all other doors found at the site so far.

The south room measures 2.6 by 1.8 meters. It had at least six jar handles mounted into its walls, four for tying the door, as mentioned above, and others for various other purposes. We found no direct evidence of those other purposes, but they may have included suspending small containers, mats as partitions, and other things.

The most prominent internal feature of the south room is a circular maize crib (Figure 6–3) with a maximum diameter of one meter. It was made of small (one centimeter diameter) poles extending upward over a half meter, probably tied in pairs, and full of maize on the cob that had been husked. Leaves were placed in various layers perpendicular to each other on the bottom, probably to form a moisture barrier between the maize and the moist clay floor. A similar multilayering of leaves separated the pile of beans from the floor of the kitchen in Household 1. The crib held at least a half-cubic meter of maize, and a rodent was found among the contents.

Figure 6–3. Parts of the vertical poles of the maize crib and ears of maize inside. These were preserved as hollow spaces in the volcanic ash, as the organic material decomposed after the eruption. We poured dental plaster in the cavity, and then excavated the volcanic ash away from the set plaster.

The roof of the building was supported by a series of vertical, horizontal, and sloping members, with grass thatch on top. It is estimated to have covered some 26 square meters in total (4.5 by 5.8 meters), of which 7.4 square meters are inside the walls. Almost 70 percent of the area roofed by the grass thatch was outside the walls.

Most bajareque structures at Ceren have more roofed area outside the walls than inside, but usually not quite so high a ratio of outside-to-inside as Structure 4. A few structures are at the opposite end of the spectrum, where the thatch roof extends only a short distance beyond the walls. All of those are the special buildings discussed later in this chapter: Structures 12, 9, and 11. Structure 9 apparently is a sweatbath, and its thatch roof protected it from the elements but did not extend far beyond its walls. Structure 12 was a very special building, perhaps the location where a shaman practiced, and its roof barely extended past the walls. The roof of Structure 11 was very thin and extended only a short distance past the thatch walls; it evidently was constructed with ventilation in mind, because of the hearth within and the need to let smoke escape. It had no earthen walls that could be damaged by the rains.

A large, solid adobe step was located on the north side of Structure 4, which was later incorporated into a raised floor area just outside the north pole wall. That elevated extramural surface extends around the northeast corner of the building. A metate elevated on its horquetas was found at the northwest corner, under the eaves. The grinding surface was about 60 centimeters above the floor, notably higher than the mounted metates of Operation 1. The woman who was the principal food grinder of Household 4 may have been taller than her counterpart in Household 1. The metate's matching mano has yet to be found. When the structure to the northwest is excavated, it will be important to see the relationship of the metate to the two structures and to the walkway between them.

The artifacts, portable features, and organic items preserved in Structure 4 clearly indicate its function as a bodega. We begin the detailed consideration of the artifacts in the north room, followed by the south room, and then other areas near the building. Some of the artifacts in the north room were found on the floor, but most were stored high on the elevated shelf. Three pots were found on the floor on the west side, one of which contained organic material that is yet to be identified. The floor's east side was kept free of artifacts. A red paint splotch on the floor evidently was a paint spill that largely had been cleaned up, but some penetrated down into the adobe surface.

The bulk of the north room artifacts was associated with the shelf; most of the artifacts were sitting on top of the shelf, but some may have been suspended below it, some could have been suspended above it, and some were in the thatch roof above it. Ten pots were with the shelf, including a ladle incensario, two polychrome bowls, two polychrome tripod bowls, four scraped slip jars, and an open mouthed bowl. One jar was full of cacao seeds, and another held a yet-to-be identified organic material. The shelf also held a piece of a finely woven cloth, a bone needle, a possible bone awl, and some pigment. A few pieces of laja that were thermally fractured during the roofing fire ignited by Unit 2 may have functioned as caps to vessels. Many chiles, apparently stored dried in hanging bunches, were scattered in the north room. They probably were tied to rafters. One obsidian blade was stored in the roofing thatch. It broke during the eruption and roof collapse, and the two pieces were 50 centimeters from each other, indicating some turbulence and item displacement.

A few items fell just north of the north room but probably were inside it before the eruption. They include a scraped slip jar that was on the shelf or suspended from the roofing and two obsidian prismatic blades that were in the thatch. A total of 14 hemispheres of wood ash were found in the north room, just beyond the room, or around the northeast corner of the building. They are generally or approximately hemispherical, as wood ash was collected from the hearth and placed in a spherical organic container like a gourd until it was about half full. Most are between eight and 14 centimeters in diameter. They seem to be common bodega items, as a dozen were found in the Household 2 bodega. Why none were found in the Household 1 bodega is unknown. The wood ash probably was added to soaking maize kernels to soften the shell prior to grinding, as mentioned in the previous chapter. They would have had to collect wood ash into these gourds, when the fire had completely gone out. If there was even an ember burning, it could catch the thatch roof on fire and burn the structure down.

Although this may seem obvious, a friend of mine in Boulder burned his house down by putting wood ash from his fireplace outside his house on a windy winter day. A hot coal blew into the woodpile and ignited the wood and then the house.

Much of the floor area of the south room is covered by a woven mat, measuring some 1.3 by 1.5 meters, with five jars placed around its margins. The mat was probably placed on the floor to make sitting on the floor more comfortable. We are used to living in a world with furniture, but it was their custom to sit on architecture: floors, benches, porches, and the like.

The south room contained numerous artifacts, some on the floor and some elevated. A total of 12 ceramic vessels were on the floor, of which nine were Guazapa scraped slip utility vessels. Six of them had no identifiable contents, but a rodent did get into one. Of the three with recognizable contents, two contained cacao seeds, as identified in the field. One of them had a mixture of cacao and another small round seed and nut shells, and the pot apparently was covered with a layer of fine cotton cloth woven as a cheesecloth or gauze. The rodent found inside that vessel is evidence that the cloth was not sufficient to keep intruders out. One other vessel contained a pointed deer antler tool that could have served as a maize husker and grain remover, as still is done in many areas of rural Central America today.

Another floor-contact vessel was a polychrome cylinder vessel that apparently held a liquid, indicated by the yellowish stain at the bottom that leaked between the sherds and onto the floor when the vessel cracked during the eruption. The yellowish color may be an indication that it was a water and maize drink, perhaps chicha, the fermented maize beer. The cylinder vessel had two identical nested polychrome bowls placed upside-down on top of it, to cap it. The bowl in contact with the vase still retained the finger swipes of food from the last person to use it as a serving vessel. This is very similar to the polychrome serving bowl with finger swipes found in the niche of Structure 2. The difference is that Structure 2 is a domicile building, and Structure 4 is a bodega. It is curious that they would have left dirty dishes in the back room of the bodega, with the inner door and the front door tied shut. The eruption intervened between the serving of the food and the washing of the two vessels. This may indicate something about the time of day or night that the eruption occurred. It may indicate early evening, after the meal but before the final cleanup. It is also possible that the bodega was tied up tight for the night, and the dishes were to be washed in the morning. At any rate, the hemispherical and cylindrical pots clearly are a set of food and drink serving vessels.

Quite a few items were stored high in the south room, and they include a polychrome bowl, four lajas (including three unmodified and one shaped but unground), bunches of chile seeds, a celt (possibly hafted), a bone needle (in thatch), and two organic containers. Both the organic containers apparently were gourds. One was not painted and contained seeds, and the other was a small gourd disk that was painted red but had no contents.

The prepared floor to the east of Structure 4 was loaded with delicate and complicated organic features. The only ceramic vessel was at the north end, a polychrome cylinder vase right at the northeast corner of the building. Just south of it was a 35-centimeter-diameter basket containing beans. The basket was resting on two laja stones, likely to retard capillary water from affecting seed storage. The basket was coiled on the bottom and supported by small diameter vertical poles around the periphery.

Two adjustable fence features were found along the east side of Structure 4, under the eaves. One was opened up and leaning against the east wall of the building, and the other was tightly coiled up and tied in a bundle. Both were made of small poles that were tied together in pairs, evidently using agave fiber two-ply twine. The height of the fence is unknown, as only the bottom portion was preserved. It was 2.9 meters long, but at the time of the eruption only 2.1 meters was stretched out straight. The remainder was coiled up at one end. The coil was around a pair of larger sticks that leaned against the edge of the building and anchored the end of the bin. It is possible that it was used to store beans, as many beans were found in this area. If it was used for beans, it was a very adjustable storage facility. Thus, when there were more beans to store, the spiral was unwound. When there were fewer beans, the fence was wound around the end sticks to tighten the bin. Another fence roll apparently was not being used, as it was carefully wrapped up in a bundle of leaves and tied with a string in a loop knot to form a tidy bundle and left near the other bin. If we are correct in dating the eruption to the growing season, this would be the time of the year when grain stocks were getting to their annual lowest point. They had stored grains for most of the year, and they were a couple of months from the second maize harvest and a bit longer from the bean harvest.

A few things had been stored above the floor in this area just outside the eastern wall. Already mentioned are the three hemispheres of wood ash that were found near the northeast corner of the building. It is almost certain that the wood ash was stored in gourds, but the gourds (and their painted surfaces) disappear to virtually nothing unless extraordinary conditions assist their preservation. That the wood ash concentrations found in this structure and elsewhere at the site are consistently hemispherical, or close to hemispherical, probably indicates that storage in gourds was a standard procedure.

Many carbonized beans were found above the basket mentioned previously. They were covered with roof thatch and had come down with the roof. Some string was found below the beans and may have been part of a net bag that was suspending the beans immediately below the thatch roof before the eruption.

Only a small area was excavated to the west of the structure. Some sherds were associated with seeds that were field identified as pipian. The sherds probably were from a jar that was resting on the west wall or hanging from the roof just outside the structure, and the seeds probably were inside it. There were no floor-contact complete artifacts; this area apparently was kept clean as a walkway.

Figure 6–4. An agave ("maguey") cactus plant in the garden south of Structure 4, with two other plants in the background. As with the maize, this was preserved as a hollow cast in the volcanic ash; we filled the void with dental plaster and then excavated the ash away. The agave leaves were used to make twine and rope, and a piece of rope was tossed onto the leaf at the lower right. It loops over a leaf.

A zone to the south of the structure was kept clear of artifacts and plants. About 2.5 meters south of the building was an agave ("maguey") garden (Figure 6–4) consisting of some 18 plants. They continue into the unexcavated area to the east and west. All have tall central stalks or inflorescences, long leaves, and places where leaves are missing. Evidently, the leaves were cut off and processed into fiber for string, twine, and rope. We have found numerous artifacts that probably were used in the de-pulping of the agave leaves to liberate the fibers. The most common are obsidian scrapers; every household had at least one, and most had a few. In addition to the obsidian scraper, Household 4 had a bone scraper that also would have been effective. One plant close to the structure had two pieces of two-ply twine draped over a leaf; it could have been thrown out as trash or blown against the plant during the early stages of the eruption. If made of agave fiber, it represents the full cycle of growing the plant, removing the leaves, de-pulping, making twine, and then ending its use.

Other plants were growing in the garden. One is identified as guayaba, and some guayaba fruits and seeds were found nearby. About two dozen sherds, clearly trash, were found in the garden area. One was lodged in the juncture between two agave leaves. Some large branches had been blown off trees to the west of the structure by the eruption and had landed in the garden.

In summary, Structure 4 clearly functioned as a bodega. An impressive range of grain storage techniques were employed, including drying and hanging, storage in pottery vessels, storage in a permanent crib, storage in adjustable features, and storage in suspended and floor-contact organic containers such as baskets. As with the other bodegas, less than half of the fired clay vessels were directly placed on the floor. The others were on the big, high shelf of the north room, on walltops, up with the rafters, or suspended from roof beams with rope. The garden of agave plants evidently was supplying raw material for cordage on a regular basis. The excavated evidence shows a great demand for cordage to fasten roofing members, to make walls and shelves and doors, to suspend pots and hang a variety of seeds and organic containers, and to make grain storage facilities. A wide variety of grains was being stored, including maize, beans, cacao, guayaba, pipian, and chiles. Future work needs to be done to set the structure into a functioning household complex, as the domicile, kitchen, and other buildings remain unexcavated.

SPECIAL STRUCTURES

A big communal building (Structure 3), a probable sauna (Structure 9), and a complex and fragile building (Structure 12) are considered in this section.

Structure 3 Andrea Gerstle (1989) was the field supervisor for the excavations of Structure 3, the largest building yet excavated at the Ceren site (Figure 6–5). It is eight meters long, five meters wide, and is over 3.5 meters tall at the rear. In spite of the size of the structure and the massiveness of its solid adobe walls, it had a striking lack of artifacts. The disparity of architectural size and artifact frequency can be expressed by the fact that many structures with less than one-quarter the floor space of Structure 3 had more than ten times the artifacts. Another way of stating it is that many other structures had 50 times the artifact density of Structure 3.

First, we will look at the structure in terms of adobe architecture with its thatch roof. Then we will look at the artifacts found inside it and near it. Finally, we will try to look at the structure and its artifacts within the functioning site.

The first suspicion that there might be a structure at this location emerged during the geophysical survey at that area, using ground-penetrating radar and resistivity in 1979 and later re-checked by resistivity in 1989. A quite pronounced M-shaped anomaly showed up in the resistivity data, indicating an increase in resistance as one approaches the structure, dropping dramatically, rising again, and then finally flattening out to join the background reading of the site. It is tempting to interpret this as an increase in resistance as the moisture decreases near the building, because the tephra layers are sloping and thus shed moisture. Certainly a decrease in moisture results in increased resistance. And it is tempting to see the building itself as catching moisture and also helping to conduct electricity

Figure 6–5. Architectural reconstruction of Structure 3, a communal building for the site, or at least for the neighborhood. Note the ample porch and the bench inside the front door. The walls were of thick, solid adobe, and the roof was supported by poles that were not incorporated in the walls.

through the fired clay platform, thus creating the strong dip in resistivity in the middle of the "M." However compelling this logic seems, we are not confident that we understand all the variables that are being measured in our resistivity traverses, and the subsurface electrical reality may be somewhat more complicated.

The anomaly in the radar imagery that was later confirmed as Structure 3 showed up as a large bulging of tephra layers above the building and a strong reflector that we now know as the floor of the building. That was seen in the rough imagery, without having to digitize and clean it up. The combination of the resistivity and radar anomalies indicated to us that this was an anomaly that needed investigation. The drill rig was placed above the anomaly, and a sample was removed of subplatform mound construction with Ilopango volcanic ash below it, and the clay-laden Preclassic soil below that. This inverted stratigraphy, as with Structure 2, was taken as confirming a cultural anomaly, such as a buried structure. With excavations, it turned out to be accurate.

A quite sizeable mound of clay was built on top of the tierra blanca joven of Ilopango, as with the other structures at Ceren. The dimensions are unknown, as most of it was covered up by the formal platform, and much of it gently slopes into unexcavated areas around the structure. It could well measure some eight by ten meters or more, and it could be more than a meter or two high in the middle, but these are guesses. The platform itself, with its vertical sides, flat top, and right angles, is an impressive construction that measures 8.2 meters long and 5.35 meters wide, with an average height of about 1.2 meters. The platform was allowed to dry and then was fired. As with most buildings at Ceren, the platform surface forms the floor of the building. One area of weakness and settling of the floor was noted, along the central axis and toward the rear (west) of the building. It is possible that it marks a subsurface feature such as a tomb or cache. It was not possible to excavate it, given the strong conservation ethic under which we are operating, and it will likely not ever be excavated. Architectural conservation is paramount, so when we excavate the volcanic ash away from a floor, step, wall, or other fixed feature, we can go no farther. This is frustrating for us as archaeologists, because we are missing an important aspect of their activities, subfloor caches and burials, if other sites in Mesoamerica are any indication. Also, we often leave sloping baulks of volcanic ash inside and outside of walls, or in doorways, to act as reinforcements where the architecture appears to be too fragile to excavate it. This also is frustrating, as we must leave some artifacts in situ or undetected, and we cannot fully record all features of walls, floors, and doorways. However, we must operate within the strictures of architectural conservation. In a very real way, the good news is the bad news. The preservation is so good that it necessitates unusual procedures that get in the way of the recovery of some data. It is an important compromise with which we have learned to live.

The rooms are defined by five walls, four of which cap the peripheries of the platform and one internal dividing wall. All walls were of solid adobe. Because we do not excavate inside of walls, we know little about the details of construction, but the walls evidently were made by the puddled adobe technique. That is, forms of wood were erected on either side of a segment, and wet adobe mixed with grass was packed inside. When the segment dried enough to hold its shape, the wooden forms were moved upward, and another segment was packed in on top of the earlier one until the desired height of wall was reached. We do not know if the walls were fired, as was the platform. After the wall was constructed, it was smoothed and then finished by the application of a layer of fine clay that varied in thickness from a few millimeters to a few centimeters, depending on the irregularities it was covering.

All walls extended about two meters above the platform. The western (front) wall was somewhat accentuated in height, as is fairly common at Ceren. It measures 2.1 meters high, while the other walls are between 1.8 and 2.0 meters. The interior wall is shorter, at 1.8 meters. The outer walls are thicker, generally thicker than one-half meter, while the interior wall is 38 centimeters thick.

A prominent cornice was constructed at the top of the four outside walls, encircling the entire structure. We can think of no utilitarian purpose for the cornice and have concluded that it was decorative and was probably placed on the building for aesthetic purposes. The cornice was quite large, 30 to 32 centimeters in height, and projecting from the building consistently 8 centimeters from the wall. We were surprised to learn that it was not built on sticks that would reinforce it by interconnecting it with the wall, but was held up only by the adhesiveness of the clay. It probably held up well under normal circumstances, but we found a number of places where the buffeting and turbulence of 50 to 200 kilometer per hour winds laden with tephra of all temperatures dislodged large pieces. Even the interior partition wall had a cornice along its western side. It projected out the same distance, but was not as tall as the exterior cornice, as it was 24 centimeters high. In both cases where walls were penetrated by doorways, the cornices continued uninterrupted above them as parts of the lintels.

The front doorway (Figure 6–6) is the same height as all doorways so far found at Ceren, 1.5 meters high. It differs in being the widest doorway found so far, 1.10 meters. The inner doorway is the same height but is more constricted at .78 meters, only slightly larger than the average at Ceren. We left the volcanic ash in both doorways because the wooden internal support for each adobe lintel has long since decomposed, and the adobe lintels would soon collapse if not supported from below. Also, the layers of volcanic ash in the doorways are mute testimony to the phases of volcanic eruptions that entombed the site.

Immediately inside both the front doorway and the inside doorway were sets of four reused vessel handles, mounted vertically as ties. Two larger vessel handles, probably from large scraped slip storage jars, were mounted in fresh, pliable adobe outside the tops of the doorjams, and two smaller vessel handles were mounted a few centimeters above the floor. Thus the door could be secured at four points. No direct evidence of either door was

Figure 6–6. The front door of Structure 3, with the volcanic ash left in the doorway to support the fragile adobe lintel. The "staining" effects of the ash layers can be seen on the adobe wall. A cornice ran around the entire building at the top of the wall. An adobe brick was used as a step up into the front room. The ample porch can be seen in the foreground, with some abrasion from foot traffic to the lower right of the adobe brick.

found; they could have been of wooden poles like the doors of Structures 4 and 7, or they could have been of matting or other thin material.

The front room had no other ceramic handles built into the walls other than the four with the doorway. However, the inner room had four additional handles in two corners that could have been used for suspending dividers or other things.

The residents' confidence in construction was impressive. They built an adobe column base on top of the front wall and on the center of the adobe lintel above the main front door. It is a low, rectangular block of adobe evidently built to support a vertical post that would assist in supporting the roof. It would have received weight from the roof and movement during a windstorm, yet it was mounted above an architectural weak point, the middle of the wide doorway. I think that can only be interpreted as confidence that the adobe lintel could hold much more than its own weight.

Four niches were constructed in the walls (not in the benches as in Structures 2 and 12), two in the front wall and two in the back wall. The niches were very similar in size, varying only slightly from the average of 47 centimeters wide, 28 centimeters high, and 31 centimeters deep. The niche roofs were supported by horizontal poles laid into the wall and were surfaced by a fine mixture of clay. Only the northeastern niche contained an artifact, a deer bone tool that broke when the roof of the niche fell in sometime after the eruption. It had a spatulate shape, but its use is unknown.

The front (eastern) room had two very large solid adobe benches built into it, which took up most of the floor area of the room. After the benches were built, only 27 percent of the internal space of the room was left as floor, and that also had to function as a corridor connecting the front door with the door in the internal partition wall. Each bench is notably larger than any of the benches found in domiciles, and the domicile benches occupy less than half of the areas of their rooms. Also, domicilary benches are always in the back, innermost room, in contrast to these two benches. These architectural differences, when combined with the artifactual differences, indicate that these benches served different functions than did those in domiciles. After finishing the discussion of architecture and artifacts, we will come back to the use of these benches.

A long porch was constructed along the front of the building. It is only slightly shorter than the building, measuring 7.88 meters, and it averaged 1.1 meter in width. It apparently was built after the structure and might be a later addition or remodeling. Only trenching could tell if there has been remodeling in this area, and that is forbidden by our conservation strictures. At three places along the edges of the terrace, erosion from foot traffic was discovered. These traces varied in intensity, and they give us direct evidence of variation in foot traffic in and out of the building. The most foot traffic exited the building and headed slightly to the left, toward the east. The second most traveled route exited the doorway and headed sharp left, hugged the front wall, and slipped down around the corner, heading west. The least traveled route headed sharp right out the door, slipped around the corner of the building, and headed west. Although expressed here as foot traffic leaving the structure, certainly that was balanced by an equal amount of traffic reversing those routes into the structure. These traces of foot traffic are arrows for us, pointing to where people went as they left the building. As archaeologists, we are interested in the pattern of human movement within the site. Future seasons of work will follow their footsteps to the places east and west of the structure.

The ascent from the porch to the floor was a sizeable one, and it was facilitated by someone placing an adobe brick along the platform edge just below the doorway as a step. This is the closest we have come to finding an adobe brick being used in architecture at the site to date, even though adobe bricks have been found in storage, under the eaves of Structure 2. The brick measures 67 by 35 by 11 centimeters, and had cracked during use, before the eruption. It helped a bit in stepping up from the brick onto the floor, but more than a half meter remained to get up to the floor.

It seems ironic that the largest roof excavated so far, built to protect the largest building we have found so far, structurally was the most independent of that building found to date. Most buildings have bajareque walls that have their principal reinforcing members, the vertical poles, firmly tied in with the roofing members, providing strong interconnections. In contrast, the roof of Structure 3 was largely independent of it, being supported by tall poles sunk into postholes outside its walls. It was also supported by some vertical poles resting on top of the solid adobe walls but not penetrating down into them. There were two of these clay post supports on top of adobe walls, one in the middle of the eastern wall and one on top of the western wall. In addition to these, five other clay pedestals were found beyond the building that probably were for vertical post support. Also, one large cobble and two lajas were on the northern part of the porch, probably for roof pole support. The lajas were built into the adobe surface during construction. Thus, the primary support for the roof was provided by posts anchored in postholes and by posts on adobe pedestals, with ancillary support by posts resting on the adobe walls. In not a single place was there evidence of a building-roof structural connection, in spite of the large size of both.

The roof itself was primarily of palm thatching, with significant proportions of grass. The peak of the roof, not surprisingly, ran along the long axis, above the internal partition wall. The dimensions of the roof are unknown, as the edge of the roof has been found only on the eastern edge. The roof measures more than 11.2 by eight meters, but how much more is unknown, as some of the outer edges have yet to be excavated. Thus, the roof covered over 90 square meters, of which 40 square meters consisted of walls and the area inside the walls. Again, more space was covered outside the walls than inside.

A few lajas were placed on top of the thatch roof, on the west side of the building. They fell with the collapse of the roof, and they were thermally fractured by the burning of the roof, by the hot tephra components, or both. Why they were on the roof is unclear, but it is possible they were weighing down a section of roof that was considered prone to wind damage.

A complex framework of posts and beams supported the thatch roof. The larger wooden members were up to 13 centimeters in diameter, and the smaller ones were as small as 3 centimeters in diameter.

Given the size and complexity of the structure, it was a surprise to us to find so few artifacts inside. That was particularly perplexing since there was direct evidence, in the form of porch erosion, of many people entering and exiting the building. Only three artifacts were found in the front room, two pots and the bone tool in the niche described earlier. The pot found on the southern bench is the largest vessel found at the site to date. It is a Guazapa scraped slip vessel that is over 60 centimeters high and 65 centimeters in diameter, with a large, open mouth. Clearly it was not for cooking, grain storage, or hauling anything. It almost certainly was for keeping and dispensing a liquid, and dispensing a lot of it, given the size of the vessel. Not far away was the only other ceramic vessel found in the building, a large Copador melon stripe polychrome bowl. It was resting on top of the inner partition wall above the same bench and could have been used to dip the liquid out of the big vessel and dispense it. The Copador vessel broke during the eruption and deposition of the volcanic ash. Most of it stayed on top of the wall, but some sherds fell onto the bench.

Only two artifacts were found in the inner, back room. The only one that was in floor contact was a donut stone in the northwest corner of the room. It was resting on its edge, at a slight tilt, much like the two in Structure 6. It probably had a stick in the hole, which held it in that position while the tephra accumulated. However, we could find no evidence of that stick. The donut stone was not decorated, but it was very well formed. It had been used extensively, judging by the wear in the perforation. It probably was used as a perforated mortar, judging from a black organic residue still adhering to the artifact. It is particularly visible on the inside of the perforation and a little bit of the top. If a stick was holding it in position, and the stone was a mortar, then the stick would be the pestle. However, that seems curious, since the stick would have had to be fairly long to hold the stone in a slightly angled position, and most pestles in Mesoamerica were short. As with the other donut stone found on the porch, it was undecorated but very well formed.

The other artifact from the back room is barely an artifact. It is a very large stone, almost the size of a basketball, that had its corners pecked smooth by a hammerstone. Surprisingly, it was not found on the floor, but it had been stored up high, either on a walltop or in the rafters. We do not know why this stone was so shaped, or why it was stored up high. It crashed down early in the eruption, before Unit 3 was completely deposited.

As with some other substantial structures at Ceren, this one too had an organic container holding the Ilopango ash-water-grass mixture suspended in the middle of the back room. As discussed before, it is conceivable that a lateral blast dislodged the tierra blanca joven volcanic ash from the earlier Ilopango eruption and re-deposited it inside the building. I favor the former interpretation.

Some incised designs, or graffiti, were found on the south wall of the inner room. They are a series of lines and punctations. We have puzzled over them for quite some time and have not reached a consensus as to what they depict. One thing I have learned over the years is to be careful in interpretations of ambiguous things. Often the interpretation tells more about the interpreter than the item being interpreted. (I have enjoyed other people's interpretations that run the gamut from sexual to religious, from maps of where the gold is buried to scenes of war.) They could be nothing more than the scribblings of a bored child.

A few other artifacts were found on the porch. Two were in contact with the adobe porch surface immediately outside the front door. A Guazapa scraped slip storage jar was found resting against the edge of the platform, to the south of the front door. It had seen quite a bit of use before the eruption, as its top and two handles had been broken off, and its bottom was heavily abraded. It was still in use right before the eruption, however. Near it was a donut stone, resting on the porch and the platform. Given its position, it probably did not have a stick in it at the time of the eruption. The donut stone was a relatively small one, with significant wear and a little organic residue in the hole. This specimen likely was used as a portable perforated mortar.

A Guazapa scraped slip vessel was found on the southeast corner of the porch in highly fragmented condition. It probably fell from the roofing and shattered. This vessel is one of the few and perhaps the only one vessel that has been found in the site to date that fell before any detectable volcanic ash had dusted the surface. Also, a large sherd apparently had been tucked above and just outside the main door, within the roofing, and fell during the early stages of the eruption. This may indicate that a minor earthquake preceded the eruption.

Those are the only artifacts found in the two rooms or the porch. Around the outsides of the building were some scattered small sherds that were clearly discarded as trash, but not very many. It was maintained as a remarkably clean building.

A number of artifact categories are notable for their absence. Not a single piece of obsidian was in or around the structure. The usual pattern of people placing their obsidian knives or scrapers in the thatch of the porch or just inside above the doorway was not practiced here. All the cutting and scraping functions so common in household buildings were not done here. There were no manos or metates, no celts, no hematite lumps, no painted gourds, and no baskets. The usual suite of household ceramics is largely missing.

How did Structure 3 function within the community? It was not a part of a household, but the abrasion on the porch indicates that it was much used by local residents. Architecturally it is the only building found at Ceren so far that could have held dozens of people in its two ample interior rooms and the broad porch. Also, it has the widest doorway found to date at Ceren. Andrea Gerstle's students, from Western Michigan University, found that the area east of the porch was a hard-packed, open area that probably served as a plaza for the building. It has two very large benches in its front room, one of which has a big pot probably for dispensing liquids. The polychrome bowl on the walltop nearby may have been for dishing out the liquids. The only groundstone artifacts were two donut stones, both of which evidently were portable mortars for grinding. They may have been brought to the structure by individuals but not retrieved before the eruption.

I suspect that this is a communal structure for multifamily use. It is possible that it was gender-specific, and it was for males only. A liquid, very possibly chicha (maize beer), was dispensed from the large pot into portable containers that people brought with them, perhaps unpainted gourds. Some people brought their personal mortars and left them there for a bit longer than they had planned. It would be fascinating to know how the maintenance of such a structure was organized, as the huge thatch roof would have to be replaced every few years and walls and other surfaces re-plastered.

Structure 9, The Sauna There is no doubt that Structure 9, at the south end of Operation 2, was designed for heating—a lot of heating. But heating what, we are not certain. The most likely possibilities are people, food, or pottery, in that order. In other words, it could have been a sweathouse (sauna), an oven, or a kiln. The data we have obtained support the interpretation that it functioned as a sauna, more than the other alternatives.

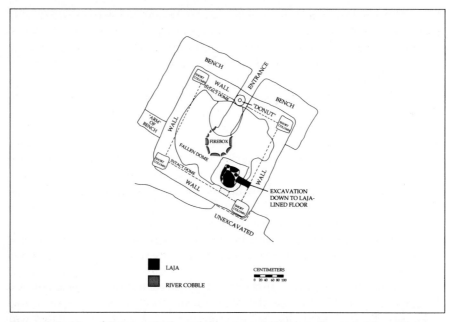

Figure 6–7. Map of Structure 9, the probable sauna. A thatch roof protected the earthen dome from rain and sun.

Structure 9 (Figure 6–7) was the third building in Operation 2 to be excavated. It was excavated under the field supervision of Brian McKee (1990), and his report is used as the basis of this section. The first two structures are the domicile and the storeroom of Household 2, but it is not clear how this structure related to that household. The first suspicion that there might be a structure at that location occurred when tephra layers were being removed, one after another, and Units 10 and 11 were noted to be bulging upward. As tephra layers were removed down to Unit 8, the bulging became more pronounced. When Units 5 and 4 were removed, the corners of the adobe structure were encountered.

The building was built on top of a sizeable clay substructure, larger than most. Then, a substantial platform was built of clay, measuring 3.8 by 3.8 meters, rising a half meter above the original ground surface. Instead of having an adobe top surface like all other known platforms at the site, the top of this platform was made of laja stones laid in a clay mortar, at least in the southeastern area. This surface forms the floor inside the structure. A one to two centimeter thick surfacing of volcanic ash from the Ilopango eruption covered the laja floor. The building is oriented 30 degrees east of magnetic north, like most structures at the Ceren site.

Short, thick walls of solid adobe were constructed on top of the platform. They are a meter high and some 35 to 40 centimeters thick. The walls are capped by a large cornice. The cornice was 27 centimeters high and 7 centimeters thick, and thus is only slightly smaller than the cornice on Structure 3. The corners of the structure have short column bases of adobe. Those square column bases provided support for a thatch roof.

The building had two roofs, one of adobe and one of thatch. The roof that was built directly into the building was an architectural masterpiece, an impressive round bajareque dome (Figure 6–8) rising some three-quarters of a meter in the middle. It was reinforced by varas 1.5 to two centimeters in diameter every 20 centimeters. It was somewhat thicker than many bajareque walls at the site, being 10 to 15 centimeters thick. The domed roof of clay was a significant engineering accomplishment and a big surprise to us as Mesoamerican archaeologists, as we had no idea that they had this technical knowledge. The underside became thickly coated with black soot from the burning of a great deal of wood. Above the domed roof was a thin roof of thatch, surely to protect it from rain and sun. The distance between the earthen and the thatch roof was short, probably less than a meter. The column bases directly supported the horizontal beams upon which the thatch roof was built.

The outer periphery of the dome is still in its original position. The majority of the dome has dropped down a bit but generally retains its original shape. The preservation of this marvel is so good that we cannot excavate through it. It must be preserved for posterity; but as archaeologists we need to excavate below it to see what the floor is like and search for artifacts that can reveal the building's function. Unfortunately, a lava bomb blasted one corner of the bajareque dome into tiny fragments, but this damage did provide an opportunity to excavate a small test pit down to the interior floor, providing a glimpse inside. A sizeable firebox was built of river cobbles set in clay mortar in the center of the structure. Its chamber is about 80 centimeters in diameter and 80 centimeters high, with walls sloping inward toward the top. Its outside diameter can only be estimated at about 1.75 meters. Thus, it occupies a significant amount of the interior space, almost one-third of the floor space. The clay mortar between the stones was oxidized bright orange by intense fires. The firebox chamber was reached by a narrow doorway low on the structure's north side. The entry was only 50 centimeters wide and 80 centimeters high, with two beams covered with adobe to form the lintel. This is barely enough room for an average-sized adult to crawl through. There was no evidence of a door, but that does not mean that a door was not present; it is probable that not all wooden doors were preserved at the site.

Above the entryway, on the outermost edge of the sloping dome, is an adobe "donut." This feature was carefully built into the structure. It is a circular flattened ring or disk of clay with an outside diameter of 35 centimeters and an inside hole ten centimeters in diameter. The hole was plugged with an irregular adobe chunk. With the plug removed it would have provided ventilation and thus could have assisted in regulating the internal temperature and/or smoke. Being above the firebox entryway, it could have set up a vortex or current, with hot, smoky air exiting through the "donut" hole.

An extensive and rather elegant bench encircles the structure's north end, wrapping around to continue along both the eastern and western walls. It has a short gap along the north side for the entrance into the

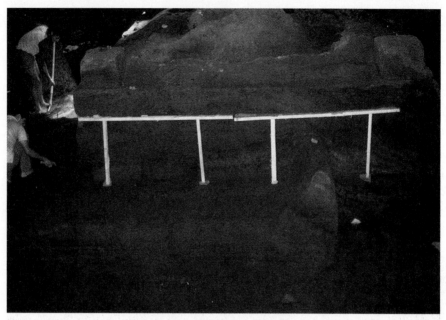

Figure 6–8. Structure 9, from the west. The elegant adobe bench can be seen, just below the wooden supports that were added to support the large cornice running around the building. The two western adobe columns and the partially collapsed adobe dome can be seen at the top.

firebox. The bench is more ample on the west side, even with a triangular arm or bench termination at its southwest corner. It certainly looks like a bench designed for reclining or resting.

Although the building is sizeable in plan view, the adobe roof is by far the lowest roof found at the site to date, and the interior space is constricted by the presence of the large firebox in the center. Around the edges of the room there is only about 1.2 meters of headroom, and in the center, the distance from the floor to the dome surface would have been about two meters. However, the distance from the outer edge of the firebox to the inside of the walls is not great and does not leave much room. The room can be entered from the north entrance. It is possible that there is an entrance along the south wall; the tephra was not removed from that area for logistical reasons, so we do not know if there is an entrance along that side.

From the evidence encountered, we can consider some of the possible functions. If it were a kiln for firing pottery, it would have been ample to process many vessels. However, pottery breaks in firing as well as while placing it in and removing it from the kiln. Kilns that are known archaeologically and ethnographically always have large amounts of broken pottery near them and at least some broken pieces inside. We did not find a single sherd inside the structure—although much remains to be excavated—and the area around the structure had few artifacts.

If the structure had served as an oven, we would expect to have some idea as to what they cooked in it. Household ovens are widespread in Middle America today. They measure about a meter by a meter, or less, and are used to bake bread in various forms. However, they are a Spanish introduction to the area, as is leavened bread. It also seems curious for either an oven or a kiln to have such a large, elegant building with the bold cornice running around the entire building and the fine bench running halfway around its perimeter. Ovens and kilns are basic, functional buildings that do not normally receive such elaborate treatment.

If the structure served as a sauna, we would not expect to see many artifacts in or around it. Taking a sauna, or sweatbath, is more than merely a way to become physically clean among Mesoamerican Indians; it has spiritual implications as well. In this light, a major architectural effort as well as the embellishments make more sense. Initially I was troubled by the amount of smoke blackening on the inside of the roof, thinking that a sweatbath would be smoke-free, but that is not so among the contemporary highland Maya. They often build a fire in the middle of a sweatbath structure, and when it is hot, they fan the smoke out and then hop into the structure. The walls retain sufficient heat to keep the inside warm. An advantage of having such a substantial firebox in the center is that the smoke could be cleared out well, yet it would retain a lot of heat. The outside bench could be used for resting while awaiting use of the structure, as well as cooling down after its use. And the river was only 100 meters east, for anyone wishing to take a dip in cool water.

Along the east side of the structure there was a zone about three meters wide that was maintained clear of artifacts and plants. The thatch roof extended over about one and a half meters of that zone, leaving another one and a half meters of open walkway. Both the area under the thatch and beyond were well-compacted by significant foot traffic. Beyond that was a maize milpa (see Figure 5–9). The milpa was not compacted by significant foot traffic. Apparently they had learned how compaction inhibits plant growth. As with most planted species we find at the site, the maize plants were encountered as hollow tephra casts around plants that had decomposed. As with the milpa of Household 1, microtopographic slope management procedures were followed by constructing soil ridges and planting on them. The maize was planted with multiple sproutings per locality. The "wavelength," from ridge top to ridge top, was about 80 centimeters. The ridges run parallel to the northern and southern walls and thus follow the spatial organization of the site. This certainly was a well-ordered landscape, with the buildings and the maize plants all lined up in the proper direction. In addition to the ridges, additional mounding of the soil often was done around the maize stalk clusters, perhaps to decrease the chances of wind throw. Maize is particularly vulnerable to wind damage because its prop roots have not kept up with its growth in size through the past few thousand years of domestication. The prop roots were exposed in some cases. These were mature maize plants, as some stalks had ears of maize in husks.

The area to the west of Structure 9 was very different from that to the east. The entire area was clay-covered as a deliberate, finished surface. A steep dip or ditch runs from the structure's southwest corner toward the southwest, and it is loaded with garbage. It contains many sherds and some chipped and ground stone artifacts. At first we thought this could be the refuse from use of the structure as a kiln, but this is general domestic trash from used and broken pots, used-up obsidian knives, and other discarded junk. It also contains maize cobs without the kernels, leaves, and tree branches. This looks like the edge of a trash disposal pit. It will be excavated stratigraphically at some time in the future to get a window on the past of the Ceren site. To date, all we have excavated existed at the instant of the eruption.

Three enigmatic laja features were found west of the structure. Each is made with a pair of laja, a rounded and smaller flat laja being placed near a larger laja that was set on edge. The larger and more angular laja is almost vertical, gently sloping back from the smaller laja at about 30 degrees from vertical. They form a partial semicircle facing roughly toward the structure. They give the appearance of being seats, as they may have been, but they would get uncomfortable rather rapidly. They could have been used by people after they exited from Structure 9.

In summary, Structure 9 clearly was designed to heat something. It is an elegant and elaborate structure, with its surrounding bench and arm, a well-made cornice running around the entire building, a very impressive dome with four adobe column bases at its corners, a domed firebox with a sunken floor and accessway, a protective thatch roof, and prepared surroundings. Not a single artifact was found inside. Had it been a kiln, I would expect to find a few sherds from firing failures inside and many broken pots outside. The architectural embellishments seem more appropriate to a sweathouse than a kiln. A kiln would work better with a clay floor than a stone laja floor, because it is not as hard and pottery breakage rates would be lower. In contrast, the moisture in a sweathouse would affect a stone floor less than a clay floor. Based on these facts, I favor a sweathouse interpretation over a kiln, but the evidence is far from definitive. I also favor a sweathouse interpretation over an oven, as I cannot imagine any food being cooked in such volume and why the structure would be so elaborate to function as an oven. In addition, there is no evidence to support its having functioned as an oven.

Structure 12: A Complex and Fragile Structure Structure 12 (Figure 6–9) was excavated during December of 1990 and January of 1991 (Sheets and Sheets 1990). It does have features found at many other structures at Ceren, including solid columns, bajareque walls, a large fired clay platform, a thatch roof, and some artifacts that were "up," such as on wall or column tops. However, the differences outweigh the similarities. It is the only building excavated at Ceren that was painted white inside and out. It is the only bajareque structure with no artifacts stored in roofing thatch. It is the only building with red paint on walls and the only one to have a window. It

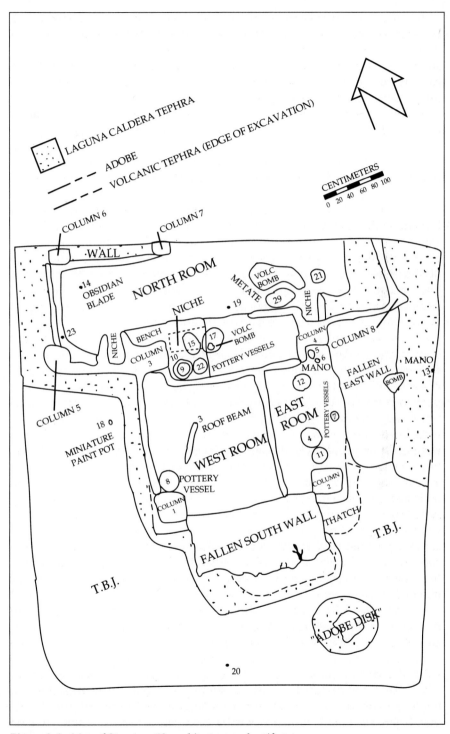

Figure 6–9. Map of Structure 12, architecture and artifacts.

is the only one to have vertical niches, and it has six of them. (Vertical niches are spaces that are enclosed on three sides; because most are associated with columns, the space is vertical.) It is the only one to have a broad spreading enclosure in front, enclosed with bajareque walls and columns, to form what we call the north room. It is the only one where access to the inner room was made very complex by many changes of direction, barrier walls, a low beam, and changes in floor level. It is the only one with an orientation 15 degrees clockwise from our magnetic directions; structures with platforms at Ceren are oriented 30 degrees clockwise from our cardinal directions. It is the only one that had a large clay disk mounted high somewhere on the south side. It has more columns than any other structure; most structures have four columns, yet it has ten (assuming symmetry). It is the only one with round cornices on the platform and the only one with Ilopango tephra in the core of a wall. The artifacts in it do not represent a functional assemblage in the way that the bodega assemblages from Structures 4, 6, and 7 indicate storage, or the household domestic assemblages indicate living areas, as in Structures 1 and 2. Rather, the artifacts in this structure may have been brought individually and left, as offerings or payment for services rendered. Many had seen considerable use. The term heirloom might apply to some. Others are quite functional, such as "chicha" pots and a deer antler tine. And some were quite used, as exemplified by an obsidian blade. The artifacts are not elegant. Many seem to have been carefully placed, such as a pot gently placed on olivela shells, and a mano on a layer of wood ash. This might have been the structure where a shaman practiced. If so, it could be considered a religious structure or shrine but not one of an organized state religion. The artifacts are relatively humble and functional and had been curated and/or used for an appreciable time. Hence, the impression is of someone receiving artifacts from local households rather than being some major pilgrimage shrine that would draw people from significant distances. Had people come from long distances, stylistic or technological differences could have been detected in their artifacts when compared to local Ceren artifacts, and the building is smaller than one would expect if it were a major regional shrine.

Structure 12 was built on top of an informal clay mound, as with most buildings at the site. Formal construction began with the half-meter high platform that measures 3.2 by 3.7 meters. Rounded cornices decorate all edges of the platform. Four columns were inset slightly from the platform corners, and bajareque walls were constructed to link them. The east, south, and west walls ran straight and directly connected to the columns. However, the north wall did not directly connect the two columns on the north side of the platform. The wall was inset to the south, creating two vertical niches to the south of columns 3 and 4.

All surfaces of the walls, columns, and platforms were painted white, apparently with a mixture of white tephra from the Ilopango eruption and a binder. The nature of the binder is unknown. Actually, the color is an off-white, or a cream-white, as the Ilopango tephra is not a pure white color. Tephra from Ilopango was also used as a core for bajareque wall construction. That probably resulted in a weaker wall than one with good quality clay-laden adobe. There may have been some kind of symbolic significance of using the white volcanic ash from the big Ilopango eruption that occurred some four centuries earlier.

A large, broad room was added onto the north end, called the north room, by the addition of columns anchoring the corners of bajareque walls. One part, the northeast corner, has yet to be excavated because of complexities in negotiations regarding property boundaries. However, if the building is symmetrical, there are six columns in the northern room in addition to the four mounted on the platform corners, for a total of ten columns.

The west wall has a window (Figure 6–10) 34 centimeters below the top of the wall. The window is 39 centimeters high and 86 centimeters long, apparently made of five sticks slanting right to left and five slanting in the other direction, in a wooden frame. The sticks and the frame were covered with adobe, smoothed, and painted white, resulting in a lattice window and a rounded molding. It probably was placed there for ventilation and light, although other functions are quite possible.

Figure 6–10. The west wall of Structure 12, with the lattice window framed by a rounded molding. Volcanic ash was left as a sloping talud against the bottom half of the wall to help preserve it.

So far, all internal dividing walls within household buildings are oriented east-west. Structure 3, a special purpose building, has a north-south dividing wall. Structure 12 has a north-south internal wall, creating a long and narrow east room and a square west room. Access was difficult to the innermost (west) room. One needs to walk up onto the subplatform mound, pass through the north room, step up onto the platform and turn left, and then right, ducking through the low doorway under the north wall. The east room is long and narrow, and apparently there is a doorway through the interior wall and a step up some 20 centimeters into the west room. It probably is a low doorway, and one would also have to duck under the low, wooden beam that connected the north and south walls. Finally one would be in the innermost room.

Because of their fragility, most walls in the north room (Figure 6–11) remain unexcavated. Most have a coating of the volcanic ash still in place, to help protect them. However, in a small test to determine wall location, a broad band of red paint was discovered. Some tiny fragments of red painted wall were found in various parts of the north room, having been dislodged by the turbulence of the eruption, so it is probable that there was extensive wall painting in the north room. Excavations of the painted walls must await adjustment of property boundaries and the arrival of a specialist qualified to conserve such fragile painted surfaces.

The artifacts are unusual in a number of aspects. Most were in direct floor contact, and some were on tops of walls. Very few were connected with the roofing members, and none were in roofing thatch. They are not a household assemblage, as known from the excavated domiciles, kitchen, or bodegas. Many are very used, as evidenced by their worn surfaces. Often they were carefully placed, or cached.

Five artifacts were placed in the deep horizontal niche that was built into the bench of the north room (Figure 6–9). The niche itself was supported by a large laja that was plastered over with clay. The five artifacts are some fragments of shell, a painted pottery figurine, half of a ceramic double ring, a deer antler, and a ceramic animal head. All were quite worn, and the ceramic items showed considerable smoothing of old breaks. The figurine is female, as clearly indicated by two breasts. Its headdress and ears were largely broken off, and the breaks were rounded by handling afterward. The breasts and the ears were painted red, and black lines were painted above each ear. The ceramic double ring fragment represents half of what was two round rings attached at right angles to each other. The ring shows quite a bit of abrasion; these double rings were common in the Formative Period, and someone from Ceren may have found this as an artifact and brought it into the site. The antler tine's proximal end still has the skull bone of the deer attached. The tip had broken and had been used some more only slightly; then a small rodent nibbled on the tip and shaft. This could have been a maize husker, an awl, or both. A little animal head figurine was found in the back of the niche, broken at the neck, and then smoothed at that break. The bottoms of the incised lines that decorate the head have white paint remaining in them.

Five ceramic vessels were directly on the adobe surface above the niche. One large bowl was upside down capping a large jar. The jar had no discernable contents; it either held a liquid or was empty before the eruption. The other three were badly damaged by a direct hit from a lava bomb and were recovered as small scattered sherds. The lava bomb also destroyed the east end of the niche. The area in and above the niche, and to a lesser degree the east room, held the greatest concentration of artifacts of anywhere in the structure.

The east room has a vertical niche south of column 4, and the bottom of the niche was covered with a layer of wood ash. On top of the ash was a one-hand mano and an isolated polychrome sherd. The sherd does not fit any vessel or other sherds in the structure and evidently was brought into the building as an isolated piece of pottery, albeit an attractive one. On the floor and just inside the doorway was a medium size pottery vessel with no contents. Against the middle part of the east wall, right on the floor, someone placed a small, neat pile of beans that was not inside any kind of container. Two pots were placed toward the southern end of the room, side by side. They are small jars that are virtually identical to the "chicha jars" that are still made and used in rural El Salvador today. The southernmost jar was gently placed on top of four olivela shells. This vessel had a human face modeled on its neck.

Figure 6–11. Looking into the niche in the north room bench, under the large laja that forms the roof (top of photo). To the right of the scale, which is 15 centimeters long, is a ceramic ring, and above the scale is a female figurine made of fired clay. Just beyond the figurine is a part of the inner skull bone of a deer; the antler tine is attached but cannot be seen because it is behind the figurine.

The west room had only one artifact, a large open-mouthed bowl in the southwest corner, in direct floor contact. It would have functioned well in dispensing liquids but not in long-term storage of liquids or solids.

Elsewhere, around the structure a few artifacts were encountered that likely had been in contact with the structure but were dislodged by the eruption. Small pieces of shell were found in the north room and to the south of the structure, in tephra, but not associated with thatching or roofing members. They likely were on walltops. A beautiful miniature paint pot was found at the juncture of Units 1 and 2 and 75 centimeters southwest of column 3. It likely was on top of column 5 or the nearby wall and was pushed off by the turbulence. It still has some bright red pigment inside it, and on its rim. A well-formed, long mano was found at the interface of tephra Units 3 and 4, 1.20 meters south of column 8. It likely was on top of that column or the adjoining wall and may have been dislodged by the final gasp of Unit 3 arriving. It ended with a strong lateral blast.

In summary, Structure 12 is highly unusual architecturally and artifactually. Most buildings at Ceren had large numbers of artifacts suspended from the ceilings or on elevated shelves, but Structure 12 had none. All walls and columns were painted white, and some were then painted red. The building does not follow the standard 30 degree east of north orientation of the site. It is the only building with a platform to divorce itself from that organizational canon. The principal inner room is difficult to access. The floor levels are quite variable, and doorways are narrow and low. There are numerous vertical niches associated with columns. The artifacts are individually placed, and some seem to have been in people's possession for some time. It is the only building excavated to date with a window. It is a lattice window inside a rectangular frame. The structure may have been the location where a shaman practiced, though it is not the dwelling of a shaman. The shamanic tradition still continues in Central America, and it is a rare town that does not have at least one. They are employed to predict the future, determine the best days to go to market, get the spirits on one's side, or assist in curing illnesses.

SUMMARY

The four structures we have examined in this chapter are extremely variable. Certainly the most familiar is Structure 4, the bodega for what surely must be a household living on the west side of the Ceren site. It is a well-constructed bodega, loaded with stored grains. The family was doing rather well, judging from the number of vessels and other artifacts, the amount of cacao in the building, and the quality of construction. They certainly had a wide variety of techniques and facilities for grain storage. And what a wonderful find was the discarded twine that got stuck on the agave leaf, representing the full cycle from growth of the leaf to manufacture of twine to use and discard.

The massive Structure 3 must have been used as a community center, or at least a multi-household communal building. The big benches in the front room, the expansive porch, the large liquid-holding vessel, and the striking lack of other artifacts argue for it having been a communal structure.

An architectural gem is Structure 9, clearly designed for heating something. It most likely is a sweathouse. Although it was a squat, strong building, it has its grace in a large three by three meter dome that rose to about two meters above the floor. Its architectural embellishments included a bold cornice atop all four walls and a bench that wrapped half way around it.

One of the most difficult structures to interpret is Structure 12. It is loaded with niches and columns and has artifacts that appear to have been brought to it individually, rather than being a part of a functional assemblage. It could have been the structure where a shaman or the like was practicing. It is so different in so many ways from the other structures that it probably functioned very differently as well. window !

7

The Site in Perspective

The previous chapters were primarily descriptive, with interpretive material secondary. In this chapter we look at the site from different aspects and emphasize artifact categories, interpretation, statistical comparisons, generalization, and synthesis. Because the site has been excavated only a few seasons, all of these interpretations are based on limited data, and this monograph is written with the understanding that they are the best that we can offer at present. As we excavate more buildings, artifacts, and other things in future field seasons, interpretations change. However, it may be a decade or two before the final words on Ceren are penned by our research team. Certainly at this point we have learned a sufficient amount about household affairs at the site to warrant writing this volume.

An example of the ongoing research is dating. We, as archaeologists, must know how old something is before we can relate it to other artifacts or sites. When I first saw the site, the excellent preservation led me to think it probably was recent, so I began to look for items such as glass, plastic, or metal. When I began seriously to entertain the possibility of it being prehistoric, I turned to the tried and true technique of radiocarbon dating, and submitted numerous large samples. As more samples are analyzed, the dating becomes more reliable. Because the analytic process results in a statistical estimate of the true age, each date comes from the lab with a central figure and a range, such as AD 590 plus or minus 90. What that means is the true date is estimated to be within that range extending 90 years on both sides of that central date, with a two-thirds probability. In other words, the true age of the sample submitted has two out of three chances of actually dating to the time span from AD 500 to AD 680. If one doubles the range, the probability becomes 95 percent, which means there are 95 chances out of 100 that the true age is between AD 410 and 770. That range was figured by subtracting 180 (two 90s) from AD 590, and then adding 180 to AD 590. This example is not imaginary; it is in fact the composite radiocarbon date established by averaging a large number of individual dates. The two-thirds probability that the site dates to between AD 500 and 690 is reasonable, given the artifacts we found, compared to other southern Mesoamerican sites that also are radiocarbon dated and dated by other means. Almost

every season we take some more radiocarbon samples and have them analyzed to further refine the dating. This may seem like an imprecise technique, because it results in a range with a probability estimate, not a specific
year date. That is true, but without radiocarbon dating it would be difficult
or impossible to obtain reliable estimates of true ages of many sites.

Fortunately, we can take advantage of the exceptional preservation
at Ceren to try to date it to finer intervals. It is a delicious archaeological
irony that we can only estimate the year when Ceren was entombed, within
a rather large time block, but we can date it to a particular season, and we
are now working on dating it to a specific time of day. In other words, it is
ironic that the smaller the time interval, the more accurate we can be at
Ceren. Dating the site to season has relied primarily on the growth of annual plants. Most of the maize plants found in the milpas of Households 1 and
2 were mature, with some stalks doubled over so the ears could dry in the
field. All milpas and gardens found to date apparently were not irrigated,
so they were dependent on the rainy season for growth. In one area south
of Household 1 there were some juvenile maize plants that probably represent the second planting that is begun in August. The analyses of other
annual plants by Maria Luisa Reyna de Aguilar, the director of the Jardin
Botanico, has indicated that they too are a mid-rainy season assemblage,
indicating August or early September. We also looked at the lower units of
volcanic ash from Laguna Caldera under the microscope to see if it contained pollen. Plants in tropical areas pollinate profusely during the dry
season, and an eruption would pull pollen down in the moist ash, particularly of Unit 1. It did not contain pollen, so we again reasoned that it was
the rainy season. It now appears that the Laguna Caldera eruption most
likely entombed Ceren in the month of August.

Because of the excellent preservation of activity areas, we have
begun looking for information about whether the eruption sealed the site
during the daytime or nighttime. In traditional Mesoamerican villages, daytime is when the agricultural implements are being used in the fields, the
hearth is burning with a pot on top, and crafts are in process. Then, the
evening meal is served, things are put away, the dishes are washed, the fire
in the hearth dies down, the mats are unrolled on the benches, and the
household goes to sleep. Within this diurnal/nocturnal cycle, where do the
data that we have found so far fit the best? It seems to be evening, after the
implements have been brought back from the fields (e.g., the digging stick
in Structure 1). But it was not so late into the night when the people were
sleeping, as the mats were not rolled out on the benches in the innermost
rooms of domiciles. The bench in Structure 1 still had four pots on it that
would need to be placed on the floor in that room, or another convenient
location. Some dirty dishes in Households 2 and 4 had yet to be washed
from their last meal. Polychrome hemispherical serving bowls with finger
swipes were found in the niche of Structure 2 and in the back of the bodega
of Household 4. I think it is indicative of time, too, that the main hearth of
Household 1 did not have a pot on it, and the fire was small, judging from

the small amount of wood and charcoal. Usually in traditional households during the daytime a fire is kept going and a pot on it, always cooking. During the night it is allowed to die down but then is fanned into action by females right after they rise in the morning.

In addition to being asked how old it is, one of the most common questions asked about the site is "have you found any human remains?" The answer is, "not much." We did find a burial of someone who died some time before the eruption; the body was buried under one side of the male workshop of Structure 5. The bulldozer had removed the head down to the hips, leaving only the leg bones. In addition, toward the end of the 1990 season, we found a hollow cavity that was a person caught by the eruption. The body was found in Unit 3 tephra, on the low hill overlooking the river. We did find three human molars in the cavity but have not yet been able to explore the cavity. We did not continue excavations in the area, as there may be more bodies there, and further work must await the arrival of a team of forensic medical specialists. It would not be surprising to me if people headed toward the river early in the eruptive sequence, as the Unit 1 tephra would have caused skin blisters because it arrived at the scalding temperature of boiling water. Unit 2 was hotter still and caused fires in the roofs of structures. It is possible that people desperately sought relief in the cool water of the river.

A DOUBLE RICHNESS

There is a double richness to the Ceren site. One richness is in how thoroughly we can see what the inhabitants' lives were like. The site provides an unusually clear window that we can peer through to see what family and village life was like 1400 years ago. The eruption hit so quickly that people did not have time to remove their most valued belongings. Thus, this is one of the few sites in the world where full household inventories of artifacts, along with stored grains, plants, insects, and rodents, are preserved. Usually, sites are devastated by the inhabitants and later residents taking all valuable items, and then the rain, sun, and the forest take over. Archaeologists are left a greatly diminished record of human activity, and they are often frustrated in what they can learn. In contrast, we can see where and how the residents preserved foods, how and where they processed them into meals, and how they built their various structures.

The other aspect of richness is in the inhabitants' terms. They had ample housing, varied techniques for grain storage, nearby gardens and milpas, and a well-developed aesthetic sense. So often they went far beyond simple functionality in their artifacts and structures and showed a desire for beauty. Bold squared cornices decorate many buildings, and delicate rounded cornices decorate the enigmatic Structure 12. Their storage vessels are decorated with sweeping multiple lines, even though it does not improve their function. Their food serving vessels are beautiful polychrome bowls, and drinks were served from polychrome cylinder vessels. Hitherto unknown was the range of gourds. Some were undecorated and evidently used to collect large amounts of wood ash and store it up in the rafters. Many gourds were painted, inside and out, with red paint being the most common, followed by green, yellow, and other colors. Some gourds were polychrome painted with bold designs, and apparently they were used for food, probably for serving individuals. They were commonly found in bodegas, domiciles, and kitchens.

Chipped stone tools received little decorative treatment, but their importance was in edge sharpness. A fractured obsidian edge is sharper than any steel edge presently available to any surgeon in the world today. In fact, it is sharper than the sharpest cutting edge in the world today, the diamond blade. Diamond blades, only three millimeters long and costing many thousands of dollars each, are used in special operations such as eye surgery. It seems anachronistically ironic that everyday residents of Ceren had sharper cutting edges 1400 years ago than do surgeons today, even in the specialized areas of microsurgery.

Their grinding stones, like cutting stones, were primarily functional. The manos and metates were probably made within the family, or made by one family and exchanged from household to household, as they are not technically difficult to manufacture. They were made of locally available materials by pecking and grinding. Even the perforated stones that we call "donut stones" were evidently made locally. Some of the donut stones were used as digging stick weights, and some may have had other functions, but most seem to have been portable grinding stones. I would love to know what they were grinding in them, whether it was hard nuts for food, medicinal materials, drugs, or whatever. Each household had a stone axe for wood working, for tasks of cutting and shaping poles for bajareque walls and roof supports. Stone axes were made of imported materials, hard greenstones like jade, that probably came from the Motagua source in Guatemala some 150 kilometers away. They probably were made by specialists outside the household and thus would have been "expensive" for the Ceren residents.

We should avoid the tendency to paint a picture of a kind of "golden age" where everything was rosy. There must have been problems, and we can see some of them. Clearly one scarcity was agricultural land. Each household had a kitchen garden where they grew essential and valued items such as agave for string and rope, cacao, flowers, and other items. They also had a milpa nearby where they grew maize. But they could not grow enough in their fields contiguous to the household to support the family for a year, and thus most of the food produced needed to come from fields outside the village. This required a significant amount of walking time, and one cannot look after the crop in distant fields as well as in the closer fields. Another problem was that once the grains were harvested, there were many little hungry mouths beyond the household members that tried to get into the food. Every structure's roof had at least one mouse, and bodegas had a half dozen. Some mice also were found on the floors or even in the storage vessels in buildings. Two species of ants have been found inside storage vessels. So, in spite of people's best efforts, there was food loss after the harvest.

Ceren residents surely faced problems from their environment. As discussed before, if the average precipitation arrived every year like clockwork beginning in the middle of May, their adaptive problems would have been lessened. But it did not, and their planting and field preparation had to cope with environmental uncertainty. Another element of the environment about which they must have been very aware is the earthquake. El Salvador is in one of the most tectonically active areas of the world, and it is an unusual month when people do not feel a significant earthquake. The architecture that we have discovered at Ceren is very earthquake resistant, probably reflecting centuries of experience, experiments, and oral tradition. The most earthquake resistant structure is the kitchen of Household 1, made of a thin thatch roof atop a wooden superstructure, thatch walls, and about 50 vertical pole supports. Even if it had fallen on someone, it would have done little damage, but it would take a tremendous earthquake to collapse it. The usual kind of construction, bajareque, is very earthquake resistant, as it is multiply reinforced from within by the tough vertical rods and horizontally with the other sticks lashed to the rods. Thus, it is very strong from within and flexible. However, all materials have their limits, and when bajareque does fail, it falls in small chunks that represent the intersections of the vertical and horizontal reinforcements. Even if one of those hit you in the head, it would do little damage, perhaps causing a scratch or raising a lump. It would not kill you, nor would the thatch roof coming down. And, structural reinforcement by the roofing supports made for a building very resistant to heavy shaking. The big adobe columns could collapse, but they would collapse outward, because an inward collapse would be blocked by the bajareque walls. The large, solid adobe walls of Structure 3 would be vulnerable to collapse during a very large earthquake, but the structure was not used for habitation, only for occasional communal activities.

Unfortunately, during the past couple of centuries in many areas of Central America, rural areas or small towns have been moving away from bajareque construction and into adobe brick construction. Rarely are adobe brick walls reinforced, and each brick weighs about 40 pounds. When an adobe brick wall collapses on people, it can do serious damage or cause death. The most common cause of death from the 1976 earthquake in Guatemala was adobe brick walls falling on people.[7] There were no deaths from bajareque structures failing. Similarly, bajareque structures fared well in the 1986 San Salvador earthquake, but adobe brick buildings failed miserably. Only the bajareque structures that had fallen into disrepair, with rotten poles or cracked walls, failed during the earthquake.

Another potential problem that needs study is possible mercury poisoning. The residents of Ceren evidently were using gourds for food containers that were painted red with cinnabar. Cinnabar is a visually impressive deep red paint, but it unfortunately is mercuric sulfide. When we find bone remains of Ceren residents, we will need to do trace elemental chemical analyses to see if they absorbed mercury into their systems, and what effects that may have had.

Another potential problem for Ceren residents was economic. They were not economically self-sufficient, either from a household, community, or regional perspective. Economic self-sufficiency can result in long-term social stability, as has been shown for prehistoric Costa Rican societies. An economy of dependency, on the other hand, runs the risk of supply irregularities. A society dependent on essential commodities from outside its territory is subject to difficulties. Obsidian, jade, and other hard greenstones came to Ceren from Guatemala to the north, and salt and seashells came from the Pacific Ocean to the west. Some of these were luxuries, but salt, obsidian, and hard greenstone axes were essential commodities. They would have required payment, probably in some form of commodity such as cotton thread or garments, painted gourds, cacao, or something else valuable, light, and thus reasonably transportable. Or, if the long-distance transported items were obtained at market in San Andres, surplus food would be suitable for payment. Household 4 could have paid in cacao. As long as the rough and finished goods were coming in steadily and the prices remained low, all was fine. However, commodities probably were constantly changing in amount and price because of factors beyond the control of local residents, necessitating adjustments to be made, thus generating uncertainty and occasional difficulties.

Thus, life was not always rosy and wonderful in prehistoric Ceren. They had their difficulties, but they certainly had advantages as well. After comparing and contrasting structures and their contents, we will return to the issue of quality of life at Ceren. As our workers have extolled, we have yet to find a single cockroach in any of the buildings, so we think that Ceren may have been occupied in a time when cockroaches were not so common. And, a life with fewer cockroaches does have something to be said for it.

HOUSEHOLD 1

We are closest to a full inventory of any household with Household 1, as four buildings and surrounding areas have been excavated. In Household 2 we have yet to excavate at least a kitchen and likely some other buildings. Household 1 had more than 75 ceramic vessels, an astounding number, in particular because it seems to be the most humble of the three excavated so far. That does not include numerous large sherds that were saved from broken ollas and converted to use as plates. That is a larger number than any of the societies surveyed by Prudence Rice (1987). She found, by looking at pottery of specific households in a number of farming cultures, that the average number of pots per household ranged from nine to 57. The pots of Household 1 are distributed as follows: 15 in the domicile, 28 in the bodega, 26 in the kitchen, and five in Area 7 under the eaves of the domicile, with a few others to the east.

We expected to find the largest storage jars with handles (large, movable storage containers) in the bodega, yet they were in the domicile, along the south wall. Thus, Household 1 maintained a micro-bodega in its domicile, in contrast to Household 2. Our working assumption here is that storage jars with handles are more movable than storage jars without handles, and smaller storage jars are more movable than large ones. The kitchen had a large number of medium-sized jars with handles, the most transportable storage containers. Open bowls of the quotidian (everyday) type without polychrome painting, which were used in food preparation and cooking, were kept in the kitchen and the bodega. They probably broke fairly often, given their use, and they probably were being stored in the bodega for easy replacement when one broke in the kitchen. The greatest concentration of storage jars without handles was in the bodega, evidently for relatively permanent storage. Polychrome painted food serving vessels were found in the domicile, bodega, and kitchen, a widespread distribution that indicates this type was moved about within the household during everyday activities. Food was stored in one place, prepared in another location, and consumed in yet another, and much of that movement from place to place was in the polychrome vessels.

Household 1 had an impressive capability for food grinding, with four metates in functioning positions. Three metates were mounted on horquetas, and one was resting directly on the floor of the kitchen. Yet another metate was upside down between the postholes and lacked only the shaped posts to be mounted and usable. Only one metate had its mano on it, the well-used one on the floor. For only one mounted metate have we found the mano, a meter away from it in Structure 6. Finding six hammerstones within the household is interpreted as evidence of manufacture and maintenance of basic groundstone implements. They almost certainly were shaping and mounting their metates on horquetas without assistance outside the household, and they probably were making their own manos and donut stones. They had to trade for their greenstone celt, and this must have been one of the most "expensive" items each household had to obtain from afar, as it not only was an exotic material from Guatemala, but it also needed a degree of occupational specialization to manufacture it.

ARTIFACTS AND HOUSEHOLDS

As we look at the groundstone and chipped stone tools found in the various structures, we can begin to see a common household assemblage. Each household owned a celt and probably used it for shaping poles for posts and roofing supports, shelves, wooden pestles, and for the horquetas that held up metates, along with other woodworking tasks. Each household had grinding stones in the form of manos and metates, but they varied quite a bit in where they were placed and how much they were used. The most common location for metates mounted on horquetas was just outside a structure (bodega, domicile, or kitchen) but under the eaves. Probably that gave protection against the rain and the sun on a hot day. Household 1 had three metates mounted on horquetas that were used only slightly and one on the floor of the kitchen that was used a lot. The only other mounted

TABLE 7–1 GROUNDSTONE ARTIFACTS BY OPERATION

Operation	Metates	Manos	Celts	Hammerstones	Donuts
1	4	3	1	6	4
2		2	1		4
3					2
4	1		1		
5	1	2			

metate found so far at the site was under the eaves at the northwest corner of Structure 4, the bodega of Household 4. It is likely that more working metates will be found when the kitchens of Households 2 and 4 are excavated. However, it still remains that Household 1 maintained a substantial food grinding capability, more than necessary for domestic consumption, it would seem. Its residents also were way ahead of other households in the number of hammerstones, primarily used in manufacturing and maintaining grinding stones. It is probable that they made more grinding stones than they needed in the family, especially manos and metates, and they probably exchanged them with other households for artifacts, perhaps painted gourds.

Donut stones seem to be a standard household item, with five in Household 1 and four in 2. A few donut stones were used as digging stick weights, or other functions, but most were used for grinding organic materials. What organic materials we do not know, as they could have been used to grind food, such as nuts, or something else. Also, we do not know if they were gender- or age-associated. It is possible that they were used by males or females, but their widespread distribution within household areas probably indicates that they were not gender-associated. They usually were stored up high, generally on walltops or in the rafters, when not in active use. That probably reflects their high value to their owners.

Chipped stone tools are more consistent from one household to another, perhaps because their uses were more restricted to cutting and scraping. Households 1 and 2 had eight and nine good prismatic blades respectively. A "good" blade is one that is not used up and discarded, has sharp cutting edges, and is not broken into tiny pieces. Household 4 has only three so far, but only about one-third of its structures have been excavated, so that amount seems proportionate. Macroblades were owned by each household, most of which evidently were scrapers. Household 2 had a stemmed macroblade that was used as a knife. It must have been quite a luxury, as dozens of prismatic blades could have been made out of that much obsidian. Household 2 had a number of other luxury items, including five miniature paint pots full of red cinnabar, a set of jade beads and other beads/pendants, and a carved bone figurine.

TABLE 7–2 CHIPPED STONE ARTIFACTS BY OPERATION

Operation	Prismatic Blades	Macroblades	Scrapers	Flakes
1	8	1	3	1
2	9	3	1	
3	———	none	———	
4	3	2		
5	1			

As mentioned above, only one structure from Household 4 has been excavated. Thus, finding two macroblades, of which one probably was a scraper, is not surprising. It is likely that one of the principal tasks for a scraper was to de-pulp the agave leaves as the first step in making agave fiber twine and rope.

Operation 3, the excavations of Structure 3, is striking for the paucity of ceramics (three pots), chipped stone (none whatsoever), and ground-stone artifacts (two donut stones). That is in spite of the fact that it is the largest building excavated to date at the site.

THE ARTIFACTS OF HOUSEHOLD 2

The domicile (Structure 2) of Household 2 did not have a micro-bodega in it, as did the domicile of Household 1 along its south wall. It had only half the pots that Structure 1 had, and most of them were decorative polychromes for food serving.

The bodega had 24 ceramic vessels, only slightly below the bodega average. The pottery was similar to that in the other bodegas, except it did not have as much variation in jars with handles as did the other bodegas. Also, it was unusual in having a suite of five miniature paint pots that may well have been used in painting the outsides of gourds bright red. Gourd painting seems to be the principal use of cinnabar paint, as far as we can tell. This may have been a craft activity that formed an economic basis for Household 2, in addition to agriculture.

Household 2 lags behind Household 1 in ceramic vessels in all types of structures, but that may be because they were making them in Household 1, and thus they had a local abundance.

THE ARTIFACTS OF DOMICILES

The artifacts found in both of the domiciles share a number of features, yet they differ in some important details. Both domiciles have food serving vessels inside them, such as polychrome bowls, and they have incensarios, here interpreted as probably being incense burners used in household rituals. However, these incensarios show little or no evidence of burning in their bowls. I would be a bit more comfortable with the incensario interpretation if there was some burned substance in the bowl, and especially if it could be identified as copal incense, the primary ritual incense of southern Mesoamerica. The domiciles differ in that Structure 1 also had a great deal of food storage in its inner room, primarily on the floor, with some on the bench and some hanging above the bench.

Architecturally, the domiciles were pretty similar, with fired clay platform tops serving as the floors, columns at the corners linked by bajareque walls, and thatch roofs. Each domicile opened to the north and had a bench in the innermost (south) room. The benches presumably were for family communal activities such as eating meals and sleeping at night. The domicile of Household 1 was not as tidy as Household 2, as it had more appendaged room space and more artifacts inside. Also, it was not quite as well constructed and lacked embellishments such as a niche in the bench, and adobe slab wing walls on the porch. Evidently, the architectural expansions of Structure 1 were responses to a need for more craft production. Both the added room (Area 5) and the expanded north porch were used in hand crafts.

THE ARTIFACTS OF BODEGAS

Each bodega had between 25 and 30 pots, a consistent figure. The bodegas share a common orientation, 30 degrees east of magnetic north. They generally store maize, beans, and chiles, and they usually have a celt near their back (south) wall. The bodegas are built on top of a substantial fired adobe platform and they all have bajareque walls, usually with solid adobe columns anchoring corners. They are located to the south of the domicile buildings, and they have gardens to their south. Each has about a half dozen mice in its thatch roof and a few more in various other locations in the building. The porches can be quite active areas.

There are some unusual or idiosyncratic characteristics of bodegas. The bodega of Household 4 contained a lot of cacao, and I suspect that it was grown locally. Conditions near the river, with the moist yet porous fertile soils, would be good for cacao production. Reyna (1991) identified a juvenile cacao tree growing in the garden of Household 4, with a bud that had just started to grow out of the trunk. In time, it would have grown into a cacao pod that would have contained cacao seeds. The building has an inner dividing wall, which is not needed in a bodega, and I suspect that the building (maybe a domicile) may have been remodeled from another use.

Structure 7, the bodega for Household 2, had a number of very valuable possessions stored in its back right (southern) corner. Those included a magnificently carved bone figurine, beads of jade and other materials, and miniature paint pots.

Structure 6, the bodega for Household 1, was the most different. It opened to the east, in contrast to the other two which opened to the north. Also, it was built on a very shallow platform, and it had a full-height bajareque wall only on its east side. It had open pole walls on the other three sides, with only a very shallow course of mud daubed along the bottom. It had a duck tied inside, and it had a metate mounted on the horquetas inside. It was the only bodega without a porch.

GARDENS

Gardens were found south of the bodegas of Households 1 and 4. Agave ("maguey") plants were prominent, and they supplied considerable fiber for making twine and rope. The artifacts evidently used for extracting the fiber, obsidian scrapers, were found in all households. Other plants were growing in the garden south of Structure 6, including manioc (a root crop, field identified but not confirmed). A flowering plant was growing south of the Household 4 agave plants, along with a young cacao tree. The garden south of Household 1 was particularly rich in species, some of which have yet to be identified. However, maize, bromeliacea plants, and others were found. It is likely that plants closer to the households were more valuable, were more closely tended, and were more productive than plants at greater distances.

MILPAS

McBryde (1947) compiled ethnographic descriptions of traditional maize milpas in southern Guatemala and western El Salvador, and his summary is useful to establish a general framework of interpretation at Ceren. The clearing of vegetation from the maizefields was a male activity performed during the dry season months of January through March. Men also did slope maintenance with contour furrowing, a very labor-intensive activity. The planting of the seeds was exclusively a male activity symbolic of the sexual/mythological "planting of the seed." Planting was done in April or May, with a harvest some three or four months later, usually in August. Some communities also did a second planting in August or September with a harvest in February, if soil and rainfall conditions would permit. They would usually plant about five grains together, and then leave some 60 centimeters before planting another cluster. As the maize grew, a mound would be created around the plants to guard against wind throw. Weeding becomes the principal activity, with the milpa being weeded thoroughly at least twice during the growing season. Sometimes beans were planted at the same time as the maize, between the clumps of maize plants. Local residents in the Joya de Ceren area stated that they preferred to plant beans a month or two later than the maize, to allow the maize to establish itself. The beans that grow on a vine use the maize stalk as support. Maize requires a lot of nitrogen in the soil, and beans are nitrogen-fixing, so they are symbiotic when they are interplanted. When eaten together, they are nutritionally supportive, as maize is weak in two essential amino acids, lysine and isoleucine, which are provided by the beans.

Similar to the ethnographic descriptions of maize milpas, at Ceren maize was planted in clusters of three to five seeds about every 60 centimeters on the ridges, with some mounding around the sproutings. The ridges facilitated absorption and minimized erosion. The milpa south of Household 1's bodega was in its first month of growth, as the plants were only 30 centimeters high. However, the milpas east of Structure 9 and east of Structure 6 were mature, with many stalks bent over so the ears dangle upside down to dry in the field. This is an ethnographically known means of field storage where plant pests are not too prevalent.

ETHNICITY

One of the more difficult challenges in archaeology is determining the ethnicity of the people who lived in a site, particularly in a frontier or multicultural setting. The finding of a few portable objects characteristic of a particular ethnic group in a site is not a reliable indicator of local ethnicity, particularly when they are relatively rare items found within a different technological-artistic tradition. (Think of all the items you own that were made in foreign countries; these items do not identify your ethnicity.) However, artifacts that are locally made, are abundant, and are sensitive to ethnic differences can provide useful evidence. The use of space is one of the best indicators, as activity areas are related to architecture, particularly within the household. One of the most striking characteristics of built space at Ceren is the construction, by each household group, of a number of functionally-specific structures. That is in contrast to so many cultures around the world where a single structure is built, and functionally-specific areas are achieved by internal walls and partitions. Two nearby cultures provide ethnographic comparisons and contrasts. The Lenca (Stone 1948), who have considerable time depth in El Salvador, ethnographically were known to construct a single rectangular building and then internally subdivide it into spaces for particular uses. The Chorti Maya (Wisdom 1940) construct a number of functionally-specific buildings per household. The Chorti are the closest Maya group to the Ceren area, now being located about 100 kilometers to the north. In terms of architecture and the use of space, the Ceren residents appear to have been more Maya than Lenca. Too little is known about other possible prehistoric peoples, such as the Xinca, to make significant comparisons.

Marilyn Beaudry-Corbett, the project ceramicist, has noted that the ceramics at Ceren contain a lot of Copador type pottery, a ceramic sphere that included western El Salvador and extended to the Maya site of Copan, Honduras, and may have originated at that site. However, a close look at style and motifs indicate that it is far from a homogeneous ceramic sphere.

Ceren ceramics, including Copador, maintain a decidedly local flavor in how often they employed the melon-stripe decoration on the bottoms of polychrome serving bowls and in the use of "swimming figures" on cylindrical vessels. The ceramics show an affiliation with the Maya but certainly do not indicate that the Ceren residents were thoroughly Maya.

The chipped stone and ground stone artifacts are not as sensitive to ethnicity as are ceramics. The stone artifacts are clearly more a part of the Mesoamerican tradition than the Intermediate Area tradition, the culture area of central and southern Central America. Both industries seem more closely linked with the Maya area than with other cultures in terms of their sources of raw materials beyond the Zapotitan Valley and their technology.

This does not mean that Ceren residents were Maya in a definitive way. It does mean that they were culturally more Maya than Lenca. So, even if the ancestors of the Ceren residents were not Maya hundreds of years before they lived at Ceren, they had acculturated to the Maya way of doing things to a rather great extent by AD 600.

THE CEREN SITE IN REGIONAL PERSPECTIVE

Of course the Ceren site did not function as a village in a vacuum. Rather, it was a settlement within the densely inhabited Zapotitan Valley, with its major and minor ceremonial-political-economic centers. The Zapotitan Valley is rather representative of the broad, fertile valleys in extreme southern Mesoamerica, each with its own hierarchy of settlements. Each valley produced and consumed the vast majority of foods, firewood, thatch, clay for construction and pottery, and groundstone implements. However, each valley needed to import certain commodities, including salt, seashells, obsidian, jade and other greenstones, pigments, and a few other items. The regional trading facilitated acculturation, and the entire southern Mesoamerican region shared characteristics such as a maize and bean-based diet, pyramids and plazas in their ceremonial centers, a basic technology for groundstone and chipped stone tools, ceramic form and decoration, and other items.

Most archaeological projects in Mesoamerica have ignored or neglected the commoners, as they have focused on elite palaces, temples, and tombs. However, in addition to working in the ceremonial center, archaeologists at Copan in Honduras (Figure 1–1) have conducted extensive excavations in the peripheries where the farmers lived (Webster and Gonlin 1988). Because the farmers' houses were abandoned gradually, they were stripped of virtually all artifacts of value to them, leaving only pieces of pottery vessels and broken stone tools. Because the structures were left in the open, exposed to the rain, sun, and wind, they have badly deteriorated, but the outlines of the platforms and occasionally some stubs of walls can be seen. In these regards, they are representative of most domestic remains in Mesoamerica, and Ceren would have been similar had it not been for the sudden volcanic ash burying it. Many of the Copan structures were built on low (approximately one meter) platforms, and often buildings clustered around informal patios. The Copan household constructors shared with Ceren the determination to build on an elevated surface, a characteristic that seems to have been lost at least among contemporary rural households in northern Honduras. Other than that, Webster and Gonlin found that pre-historic Copan houses are strikingly similar to contemporary rural houses in the area. Copan and Ceren residential structures also share the characteristic of having an abundance of obsidian, in contrast to many peripheral farming households in southern Mesoamerica. The Copan structures date slightly later than Ceren, between AD 700 and 900.

Because of its sudden burial that preserved plants in fields and gardens, Ceren offers us the unique opportunity to know specifically what individual households were growing and where they were growing it. The preservation of organic materials allows us to see how they stored and processed food in the household. Also we now know how they made string and rope—from agave growing in the garden—and how they used them to tie roofing members together, to make net bags and ropes for suspending pots, to tie a duck to a post, and many other uses. The sudden burial did not allow people to remove their valued possessions, and it did not allow for later people to scavenge the site for building materials or other artifacts. In addition, the sudden burial protected the sophisticated earthen domestic architecture from the elements and from tree roots, burrowing animals, and other agents of disturbance. We had no idea that common people lived so well in Southern Mesoamerica some fourteen centuries ago.

SUMMARY

As we have excavated the various structures, activity areas, artifacts, gardens, and milpas of the Ceren site, we have been impressed with the quality of life that existed there 1400 years ago. They had ample roofed areas inside of substantial buildings and extensive areas under the eaves outside the walls. Households had astounding numbers and varieties of storage, cooking, and food serving vessels, the latter including elegantly painted gourds. They had a domestic architecture that was very well adapted to a tectonically active area. Although it is in a tropical, wet environment, averaging some 1700 millimeters of rain a year, they had sophisticated adobe architecture. They could make solid adobe walls, adobe lintels, earthen domes, suspended cornices, niches, porches, lintels, benches, windows, and other features. If Structure 11 is any indication, they had well-organized and efficient kitchens.

As we were excavating the remains of this rather impressive lifestyle, we and our workers could not avoid comparisons with contemporary life in El Salvador. In certain specific cases, our workers were able to identify things that had not changed, that were a part of a continuous tradition, such as the metates being mounted on the horquetas. They could identify with the Ceren residents using a variety of techniques to try to keep ants and mice out of their stored grains, including suspending pots from the rafters with ropes, using tight lids on pots, and constructing granaries. Sometimes they succeeded and sometimes they failed, both in the past and present. Thus, the process of excavating the Ceren site had a strong effect on people in a way far greater than excavating a pyramid or other large structure. It is difficult to personally relate to a pyramid, but it is not difficult to relate to the everyday successes and problems that families had at Ceren. The workers are discovering their family roots at the Ceren site. Our workers are immensely proud to be a part of the research team discovering such important buildings, artifacts, and the Classic Period landscape. Thus, their eagerness and excitement while working at Ceren is understandable.

On a personal level, we were not able to avoid noting that all of our workers were inhabiting dwellings that had less space in them and less space under the eaves and outside the walls than were available to Ceren residents. The workers had fewer personal possessions, had less food stored in their houses, and had fewer artifacts that were aesthetically pleasing. Our workers noted the lack of cockroaches excavated at the site and speculated that it might have been wonderful to live without having to battle those noxious insects all the time. There was an underlying sadness that their lives are more impoverished than their ancestors some 1400 years ago. I felt this every day while traveling to the site and seeing by the side of the road squatter's shacks built of cardboard, scraps of plastic, and scavenged fragments of metal roofing. I felt this every time I went into the town of Joya de Ceren, and I felt it acutely every time I visited a worker's house. This brings up the questions of why, and how?

What has gone wrong in El Salvador to cause such a decline in living conditions? I believe part of that answer lies in the relationship of people to their environment and part in the political aspects of the distribution of wealth. There is no known environment on earth that can sustain indefinite population increase, and El Salvador is no exception. Although blessed with fertile soils and considerable rainfall, the factors of environmental hazards, technology, and population limits must be taken into account to achieve a stable adaptation.

The country of El Salvador contains 21,393 square kilometers, about the size of Massachusetts. Its population has undergone drastic fluctuations during the past few thousand years, which are summarized in Table 7–3.

What we can see from these figures is that prehistoric population reached a maximum in Late Formative times, in the centuries near the time of Christ, but populations at no time in prehistoric periods evidently outstripped the carrying capacity of the environment. The population of central and western El Salvador was devastated by the immense eruption of Ilopango Volcano in AD 175, but eastern El Salvador largely escaped the disaster. Population restabilized by around AD 600, based on data from the Zapotitan Valley, to decline only slightly in the centuries just before the Spanish Conquest. The Spanish Conquest resulted in a massive depopulation of the New World on a scale that the world has rarely seen, most of

TABLE 7–3 ESTIMATES OF POPULATION, EL SALVADOR

Year	Population	People per square kilometer
AD 1990	6,000,000	280
AD 1980	5,000,000	238
AD 1969	3,350,000	159
AD 1900	775,000	37
AD 1800	175,000	9
AD 1551	55,000	3
AD 1524	400,000	19
AD 1400	534,825	25
AD 1100	748,755	35
AD 600	748,755	35
AD 300	213,930 (?)	10 (?)
300 BC	962,685	45

See Sheets (1983:9) and Black (1983:82) for more details. The Zapotitan Valley figures are cut in half to extrapolate to less fertile areas.

which was due to diseases. Smallpox, measles, influenza, malaria, yellow fever, and other diseases decimated New World Indian populations that had no resistance to them. It is an indication of the scale of that devastation that it was not until early in the 20th century that populations of El Salvador increased to prehistoric levels. The astounding population explosion of El Salvador is a phenomenon of the late 19th and 20th centuries. It is that rapid population growth that has exceeded the carrying capacity of the land and the available resources and has impoverished most Salvadorans.

It is a bitter irony that a cause of that increase was the introduction of modern medicine, hygiene, and other Western practices that decreased the death rate, as the birth rate remained high. What can only be seen as doing good in the short-term, for example, decreasing infant mortality and saving lives, ended up doing a terrible thing in the long-term, causing the suffering of millions of Salvadorans today. Many Salvadorans go to bed hungry, and they witness numerous family members slowly starving to death or suffering from malnutrition and the various disorders that accompany it. It was advantageous to the Europeans and Americans who were introducing coffee into El Salvador in the 19th and 20th centuries to have cleaner living conditions for themselves. And it was, and still is, to their benefit to have a large underemployed population that will work for very low wages in the labor-intensive jobs of picking and sorting the coffee beans. Thus, in addition to the demographic problems of overpopulation, the politics of the distribution of wealth continues to plague the country.

The richness of life at Ceren 14 centuries ago puts in stark contrast the desperation in the lives of many Salvadorans today. It is much better to make hard decisions for the long-term benefit of people and society than make short-term decisions that benefit only a few, or make things apparently better for all, but only for a relatively short time.

Epilogue
Doing Research: The Inside View

❏

INTRODUCTION

In the previous chapters I have emphasized Ceren in terms of the methods employed and the results, with interpretations and comparisons. Those, of course, constitute the nature and objectives of doing research. However, what usually gets left out of an archaeological report, whether it is an article in a journal or a full book treatment of a site, are the practicalities of doing that research. The human side of things, with the excitement, frustration, fears, fun, dangers, satisfactions, and laughter get left out. However, this epilogue is an opportunity to discuss some of these aspects of doing research in the field in Central America, from a personal perspective. I begin with the logistics of organizing and staffing the project, traveling to El Salvador, and maintaining cooperation with people in that country. I then look at difficulties in doing the fieldwork, use of certain instruments, and how we relate to people and the media. In addition, I discuss our attempts to relate with local people and our attempts to assist people in need. Finally, I view the Ceren project in relation to others, as we visit them and share research results.

LOGISTICAL COMPLEXITIES IN CONDUCTING INTERNATIONAL RESEARCH

From the preceding chapters one might think that doing archaeology in El Salvador is a matter of waltzing into the country, digging up some really interesting things, checking out what we've found, writing down information, and then returning to the U.S. Not quite. Just getting to the point that you can sink the first spade into the ground takes much effort.

One of the first things to be done is to obtain permission from the landowners and the government to do the work. It is important to understand a big difference between U.S. and Latin American culture. In the U.S. we obtain permissions with written documents, with lawyers, and with the threat of judicial proceedings to back us up. In Latin America people generally operate on a much more personal level. Important decisions or agreements are made between people only after they have gotten to know each other sufficiently to feel they could work together in the future. They need to judge character and form a working relationship, perhaps involving a friendship, prior to entering into a formal relationship of granting permission. I personally prefer their system, because it puts more emphasis on confidence and trust right from the beginning, and less on lawyers and difficult judicial proceedings. Their system invests time and effort early to try to weed out problems before they occur, and thus generally avoids a great number of complications and hassles later.

What this meant, in my case, was traveling to El Salvador every year or two during the 1970s and 1980s, to maintain friendships and acquaintances and to meet newly appointed officials and get to know them, and them me. Sometimes I was able to get some funds from the University of Colorado or other sources to do so, and at other times I paid for it myself.

Another essential ingredient for a successful field season is the permission of one's university to be gone. This is highly recommended to ensure that when one returns to the university, one's job and office are still available(!). The complexities of leaving for a semester are considerable, as alternate advising for undergraduate and graduate students needs to be set up, substitute faculty to serve on MA thesis and PhD dissertation committees need to be found, and a myriad of other details must be handled. No student should have difficulties because a professor is in the field. The classes that I would have taught need to be taught by someone qualified, and it takes time to find the appropriate person. It is a tremendous burden on the family, as my wife had to quit her job, and my daughters Kayla and Gabi were removed from their schools, home, neighborhood, and friends, for almost a year.

FUNDING AND STAFFING THE RESEARCH PROJECT

An obvious essential for international archaeological research is adequate funding. We usually spend around $90,000 for a field season of three to six months, with the money spent on international travel, room and board, salaries for Salvadoran workers, vehicle rental, gasoline, equipment and supplies, utilities, insurance, shipping, university overhead, and myriad other costs. Very few agencies, private or public, will entertain a proposal for that amount of money. The most appropriate agency for the kind of research we are doing is the National Science Foundation (NSF) in Washington, D. C., a part of the federal government. The NSF budget is only a fraction of what it should be if it were to fund even half of the research that is proposed to it. It is highly competitive, and in the recent round in which we fortunately got funded, 87 percent of the proposals were rejected.

A success rate of only 13 percent is not a cause for optimism. A proposal needs to be really outstanding, almost without flaw or weakness, to be funded. It takes many months to write a proposal that stands a chance to be approved. Many letters and telephone calls are necessary to line up the people and to have accurate and minimal costs in the budget. I have learned that one thing which really improves a proposal's chances is to have it firmly criticized and then revised before I submit it to NSF for review. One reason for the success of our multidisciplinary research in the field is that we have obtained the participation of some of the finest geophysicists, volcanologists, and conservators in the United States, but it is not easy for them to leave their intense research programs to join ours for a few weeks. The students I solicit are the best I can find. I post a notice for all students at the University of Colorado to read, then I allow them time to think and talk it over before I select the most qualified. Initially I look for the most qualified in terms of past excavation experience, abilities to analyze data and write, and abilities in Spanish. I also look for students who are more than archaeological technicians, who can understand and respect the culture of the country, and interact with its people.

TRAVELING TO EL SALVADOR

When the statistically unlikely events all coincide that we have permission from landowners, government officials, and the university, and funding of the National Science Foundation, we take off for El Salvador. When we are going for only two or three months of summer, we usually fly down, as time is scarce. That means that we have to rent vehicles within the country, and they are very expensive, 200 to 300 percent more than in the U.S. When we are spending more than three months in El Salvador, we rent vehicles from the University of Colorado and drive down. That involves a few complexities, such as legally torching off catalytic converters from exhaust systems, getting notarized permissions for all anticipated drivers for crossing frontiers, obtaining visas, and other items. The drive is about 3500 miles, which is quite a distance, but I love the experience. In classes that I teach at the University of Colorado, I talk about the ecological zones of Mexico and Central America and adaptive traditions that continue today. It is a pleasure to see the local people and stop to talk with a traditional agriculturalist about why he is contour ridging or how his harvest is proceeding. I also enjoy the break from my usual hectic pace of meetings, class preparations, teaching, telephone calls, memoranda, and so forth at the university. None of those exist on the open road. It takes us about a week to do the driving, and we avoid driving at night because of potholes, cattle on the highway, and other hazards that are more readily avoided in sunlight.

In Latin America, one has to drive with ten times the alertness that one uses in the United States, because of heavier traffic, more large animals, worse roads, and a few dozen other reasons. Accidents must be avoided at all costs, not only because of the obvious problems of injury and property damage. As soon as we cross the border into Mexico, we have entered a different system of justice. Latin America, like most of the non-English speaking world, functions on the Napoleonic code of justice. What this means is that anyone who is suspect of doing something wrong has the responsibility of proving himself or herself innocent. All people involved in a traffic wreck can be jailed until they demonstrate they were not at fault. That is not always easy. And it is always costly in time and funds. Traffic accidents are a hazard to be avoided.

DIFFICULTIES WITHIN EL SALVADOR

Speaking of hazards, El Salvador has had a hazard in progress for over a decade, a civil war. The FMLN (Farabundo Marti National Liberation Front) guerrillas have been battling government troops since 1979. Prior to that, in the 1960s and early 1970s there was a legitimate struggle for philosophy and power between opposing factions. Some argued that the best future of the country lay in improving business conditions for production and export of coffee, cotton, sugar, and some manufactured goods. Increased prosperity at the top would lead to a general improvement in wealth and living conditions for the rest of the populace. Others argued that the place to start was the bottom, with improving living and working conditions and wages of the poor. It was generally not an armed struggle but was waged on the editorial pages of newspapers, in rallies and demonstrations, and in public debates. However, as the cold war intensified and Nicaragua went Marxist in 1979, both East and West chose El Salvador as a stage for competition and fighting.

The struggle turned into an armed battle throughout the 1980s, as great amounts of arms flowed into the bodegas of both sides. The Salvadoran government received regular shipments of U.S. military equipment and assistance. The guerrillas received arms from various sources, including Nicaragua, Cuba, the USSR, direct purchases from international arms merchants, and captured government sources. Thus, winning an argument shifted from logical persuasion to violence, and the country fell into civil war. The war was waged throughout the 1980s and now into the 1990s, and the suffering wrought on the Salvadoran people has been immense. The death toll stands at almost 80,000 at the time of this writing. That is a high number for any country, but it is particularly bad for a small country. That is a much higher total number of deaths than the U.S. suffered in Viet Nam. Proportionally, that would be about two and a half million Americans dying in a war, an unthinkable toll, but it does give us some idea of how the suffering caused by the war has affected Salvadorans. That does not take into account the hundreds of thousands of injured and permanently maimed people, and all the families that have lost their lands and homes to the conflict and had to flee to seek refuge in San Salvador or in other countries. The kind of suffering from poverty, malnutrition, and underemployment is more than any country should have to bear, but to add to that, the Salvadoran people have had to live within a civil war. Most Salvadorans do not care what "ism" is running the central government, whether it be socialism, capitalism, or communism, so long as they have a decent job, some liberty, and the ability to feed, clothe, and educate their children.

Unless they are attached to one side or the other, foreigners in El Salvador have not been targets during the war. One has to be careful not to be in the wrong place at the wrong time, as many civilian deaths occur when a firefight breaks out between guerrillas and the army. We expend quite an effort to stay well-informed about troop movements, the latest hot spots, possible guerrilla infiltration, and the overt battles being waged.

COOPERATION WITH THE HOST COUNTRY

Some Latin American students have complained about "academic imperialism," where people arrive from the U.S. or other developed countries, stay for a while in their country, presumably do good work, often live isolated from natives, return to their country of origin, and publish in their own language. They leave their Latin host country with only a vague memory that they were there doing something. We have tried to avoid that by doing everything we can to publish first in Spanish in the local country. We involve local students, professors, and scientists as much as possible in the field and laboratory research and in the final publications. We have been training two Salvadoran students in field and laboratory procedures, in the hopes that they can go on to earn advanced degrees and become the first Salvadoran archaeologists. It is time that the country has its own archaeologists, instead of having to await the arrival of foreign groups to do research.

HIGH-TECH APPLICATIONS: FIBER OPTICS

Along with the best geophysicists, volcanologists, and conservators comes the need for the best instruments for their use. We have used state-of-the-art geophysical instruments with considerable success, especially ground-penetrating radar and resistivity. We are doing remote sensing using Landsat satellites to record moisture, soils, and vegetation variation in the area. We are planning overflights by NASA aircraft to take color infrared photography and use digital sensors to look for buried archaeological and volcanological features.

The Ceren site is very unusual in having cavities in the volcanic ash that sometimes are of extraordinary significance. Unlike most archaeological sites that have no such cavities, the warm, moist volcanic ash units packed around organic items, ranging from little corn plants to full size trees, from tiny seeds to large organic containers. After organic decomposition, presumably by fungi and bacteria, the item was preserved as a hollow cast in the ash. We can then mold it using dental plaster or another substance. However, when we find a cavity we must first explore it to determine what the item was and how well the surface of it is preserved. Thus, we need some means of seeing down into dark cavities, often not in a straight line. In searching contemporary technology, we have found that the best instrument available is a fiber optic proctoscope, as mentioned in Chapter 1. Without the proctoscope we would have to cast blindly, and thus waste large amounts of dental plaster on beat-up branches of trees blasted by the base surges into the site; we would not be able to adjust our techniques and materials to individual conditions of preservation. Fiber optics have helped the research at the Ceren site considerably.

THE SITE, THE MEDIA, AND THE SALVADORAN PUBLIC

While planning the 1989 and 1990 field seasons, I had to make a key decision. Would we, as I was initially thinking, keep a low profile and just go about our business? Would we live quietly and avoid the press and other ways of advertising our presence in the country? Or would we be more overt? I asked many trusted friends in El Salvador, and they agreed that we would be much better off being overt and open. The country is small enough, and we were obvious enough, that our living and working quietly could arouse suspicions, and that might be dangerous. So we decided to be very open and allow the press to visit the site, along with a tremendous variety of other groups, to learn what we were doing, how, and why. This decision did coincide with one ethical issue, and that is that we were receiving taxpayers' dollars to conduct research that was not clandestine in any sense, and thus we had an obligation to share that research with as wide an audience as possible.

We opened the doors to the press every Thursday, and they came in droves. We quickly realized that we could not satisfy the desires of all the print and broadcast media, so we limited the press to Salvadorans only, as keeping them informed is more important than audiences outside the country. I had to say no to CNN, NBC, and CBS, much to their surprise.

The diplomatic community became very interested in our research, and many times they helped out. For instance, the Italian ambassador visited the site many times. He arranged for a couple of Italian volcanologists to visit, who had done some research at Pompeii, and they were very impressed. They said that the preservation of organic materials and architectural details is far better at Ceren than at Pompeii. Other ambassadors and their staffs visited the site frequently.

The U.S. ambassador decided to visit as well, but his visit was not as simple as the others, as he has the tightest and most massive security of any person in the country. The day before his planned visit, he sent Gordon, his chief of security, to look over the place. Gordon, a young man with plenty of "macho," arrived in a flurry in his armored car. He jumped out of the car and began marching around looking at the lay of the land and the prehistoric architecture. I spent a couple of hours showing him the various excavated structures as well as possible escape routes, paths in and out of the land, and other things related to security. When he returned to his armored car, he was struck by dismay as he looked in through the bullet-proof glass and saw the car keys and his machine gun resting on the front seat. In his excitement to see the site, he had inadvertently locked them inside. He broke into a profuse sweat as his macho diminished markedly, and he began trying to break into his armored vehicle. After suppressing guffaws, we tried to help him, but we all failed. Finally, one of our workers slipped his machete between the glass and the rubber molding of the door window, tripped the latch mechanism, and opened the door. We wondered what that worker did in his spare time. The visit of the ambassador did come off without incident the next day.

Not only did we have numerous visits from the diplomatic and the press corps, and Salvadoran government officials, we also had some visits from other political groups at different times. As I would show each group around the site, I would emphasize that we are clearly non-political and doing work of value to all Salvadorans and interested people elsewhere, no matter what their contemporary political beliefs are at present. The single most common comment made by people from all political persuasions has been that the Ceren site is the most important thing that has happened in their country during its entire civil war. They commented on how they had suffered, but this was a ray of light, an island in a sea of suffering, a wonderful piece of good news amidst the awful news. At least they could agree on the importance of the Ceren site, even though they had trouble agreeing on much else.

LOCAL PUBLIC RELATIONS

We are particularly interested in maintaining good relations with people in the town of Joya de Ceren, a community of some 3000 people just south of the site. If people from the town turned against us, we could have all kinds of difficulties. In the interest of openness, we gave numerous talks in town to anyone who wished to come, explaining the objectives, the finds, the future, and the implications of the project for them. Occasionally townspeople worried that the excavations would expand southward and require them to abandon their homes. I have promised that we will never excavate in or under the town. One person, Evelyn Guadalupe Sanchez, was hired by the Patrimonio Cultural to maintain close and good relations with the townspeople, and she has been very successful. We could not have everyone from town to visit, as the site is far too fragile for thousands of people to visit. However, we did decide to invite the school children.

When Evelyn suggested we invite the schoolchildren, I agreed immediately because I really enjoy talking with the young and sharing the Ceren site with them. I neglected to ask how many there were, so a few days later, when she told me she had set the visit up for the next week, I was somewhat taken aback by her statement that 800 students were coming. She asked whether I would prefer all 800 at once, or two groups of 400! I chose the latter, as somehow it seemed a bit more manageable, and we began intensive planning, as the largest group we had had before was 30. When they did arrive, it was clear that they had been well-trained by their teachers. They came into the site single file, in a long line holding hands, and they were the best behaved group that has ever visited the site. I received more pleasure and satisfaction in giving them a tour than any other group, and seeing in them an understanding and a sense of pride in having something of that importance in their own back yard.

We saw, in Chapter 5, how the "hauling ash" program created good will with local residents by loading trucks with volcanic ash excavated at the site and taking it wherever anyone wished. We were able to create a level playing field for the school, as people were tired of playing on a slope that encouraged the ball to roll downhill toward the river. We certainly improved a lot of roads and helped a lot of patios. We also used the individual contacts created by the program to allay fears that we would excavate under their houses in town and thus force them to leave.

Some of this could be misinterpreted as indicating that we anticipated having problems with the campesinos (country dwellers) in the area, and I need to clarify that. Salvadoran campesinos are the most generous and honest people I have ever met. The place where people need to be careful with their possessions is in the capital city, San Salvador. I regularly leave cameras, money, portable computers, and other valuables in our vehicle at the site, with the workers, and they have always proven themselves to be totally trustworthy. I even gave up trying to keep track of the various loans of money that I made to individual workers, as they kept meticulous track and always repaid every cent.

Salvadoran campesinos are generous even to the point of embarrassment. One time we were doing archaeological survey in a very isolated part of the Zapotitan Valley and sat down under a large tree for shade to eat lunch. A poor family living on the other side of the tree emptied their humble house of all furniture (three chairs and a table) and brought them to us, along with the only three Coca Colas they owned. We thanked them profusely and tried to pay them for the Cokes, but they would not accept any money. Finally I did get them to accept a Swiss Army knife as a present, but they were very reluctant. It is so unfortunate that people in the capital city, Salvadorans and Americans alike, have such a suspicion of the campesinos, as it is so unwarranted.

Although the campesinos generally are poorly educated, they are far from ignorant. Rarely in the campo does someone go past grade school, and children often drop out of school in the third, fourth, or fifth grades to help the mother in the house or the father in the fields. Campesinos generate a patience and grace that is necessary in a poor third world country. They can be very articulate and insightful when they trust someone, but are very quiet and circumspect with strangers. I will never forget the statements of Señora Chuz, of Chalchuapa, when we were saying goodbye to her after having lived with her for five months, a number of years ago. We came to like her, and she us, but we had no idea how much until we were leaving. I told her, in my best Spanish, thank you very much, I appreciated all she had done for us, and wished her the best. Then she began to talk. In measured tones she described how lives are like paths. Paths do not exist as isolated straight lines. Paths cross and bring experiences and influences together that enrich all. When one is open to adventure, open to learning from others, the paths bring new insight into people and distant places. Paths are always dividing, but when one gives to others along the path and learns from them, then everyone has gained from the experience. Where paths divide, we must make careful choices, informed by what we have learned on the route. Thus, we should live life to the fullest, not by sitting and waiting for things to be brought to us, but by seeking the encounters, the paths coming together, and the paths dividing. And one should never forget that what happens along the path is at least as important as the goal that lies at the end of the path. I must admit that, as a typical male, I shed tears maybe once a decade or two. That was the time. Her expression of her philosophy of life, done so eloquently and including how much we meant to her, reduced me to tears.

TRYING TO HELP

Life in the campo often is filled with some very difficult decisions, many deriving from overpopulation and poverty. A few years ago, my wife Fran and I came across a severely malnourished infant in a humble thatch-roofed house near Chalchuapa. The appearance of the baby, about two years old, was appalling. The baby was a combination of appearing like an infant, yet it had characteristics of an old person with wrinkled skin and sunken features. It was crying with a plaintive, weak sound. The woman who was trying to care for it said, in forthright tones, that the baby was dying. A baby dying! That brought forth in me a "Gringo" reaction of having to do something, a lot, right away, anything, to save the baby. I talked with her briefly and found out that she was not the mother. The mother had abandoned it. Fran and I drove into Santa Ana where there was a decent-sized hospital. There we went to the pediatric section and talked with a doctor about the situation. He said yes, he could find a bed for the baby. Aah, I thought, this is the chance we were hoping for. He sensed this and said to sit down and think about the situation in more broad terms. If we bring the baby in and he is able to save it, it will occupy a space that will have to be denied to another baby. In other words, no matter what we do, a baby will die, and we will be deciding which. Thus, the important thing to determine is if the baby from Chalchuapa is saved, would it be cared for in terms of food, clothing, and the like, in the long run. That we could not answer without a longer conversation with the woman in the shack, so back there we went, feeling an enormous burden to make the right decision. In talking extensively with her, we became convinced that she would, indeed, care for the child even though it was not her own, so we did make the decision in favor of that infant. We took the woman and infant to the hospital, and the doctor was able to save it. The infant, in relatively healthy condition, was released to her care a few months later.

THE CEREN PROJECT AND OTHER RESEARCH PROJECTS

Another thing we do during field seasons is travel to other sites and share the results of our work with other research teams. A number of years ago we loaded up the van and headed toward the Maya site of Quirigua, in Guatemala. A group of archaeologists from the University of Pennsylvania was there, and they were eager to hear of our work firsthand, and we wished to learn from them directly. We took photographs, plan drawings, and other information of our research to share with them. We of course took no artifacts, as all artifacts that we excavate can never leave the country, by law. If there is any law that we should respect, it is that one, as the looting of artifacts from sites is atrocious throughout Central America, and many get smuggled out and purchased by wealthy collectors in the U.S. and Europe. They never see the terrible damage they are subsidizing.

Crossing the border from El Salvador into Guatemala was routine: it was awful. I don't know if there is anything I hate more than a land crossing of a Central American border. It is so much easier to fly in and go through customs and immigration at the airport. At the border there are vast numbers of officials (and self-appointed officials) who feast on the hapless traveler. Anyone who doubts the adage "power corrupts, and absolute power corrupts absolutely" should go through a border crossing in Central America. Dante, in writing "The Inferno," omitted Central American border crossings. Perhaps he decided that they were too grim for Hades. As you approach the frontier you can see drowsy officials coming to life and taking their feet off the desk. The traveler must act with total abject humility and pay all sums that are overtly requested, as even the inkling of displeasure or resistance by the traveler guarantees massive retaliation. That retaliation for sure involves many more payments of various "fees" and stamps from other "officials," and at worst they will flatly deny permission to cross the frontier. Often, one will be turned back with orders to go to their capital city to get a different kind of visa stamped in the passport, or to get other documents, particularly if that item will take several days to obtain. The traveler must never forget that the border "officials" have total power and authority, and they enjoy using it.

Often, impediments are placed in one's way as a slightly subtle way of requesting a bribe. Rarely does a border official directly ask for a bribe. I was, however, directly approached for bribes recently at a police roadblock in Guatemala. Officially, the police were doing their job stopping about every fourth vehicle and checking to see if the papers were in order, primarily car registration papers, and that the driver had a valid driver's license. We passed their careful scrutiny on both counts. However, before we could leave, the policeman in charge of the checkpoint asked if I could give him a "recuerdo" of the United States. I was a bit surprised, as a "recuerdo" is a little trinket or souvenir that travelers buy when in a distant location to take home to remind them of that experience. He clarified his use of the term right away by saying that a few dollar bills from the U.S.

would serve very well as "recuerdos" for him. Yep, that left little doubt. He was standing rather firmly between me and the car, so I decided to give him two dollar bills, which I quickly rolled up and passed him. I tried to hop in and drive off before any more "recuerdo" requests arrived, but I was not fast enough. Two others hit me up, and I gave them one each, before zooming off. I feigned ignorance of the other three who were rapidly walking toward me also requesting "recuerdos," and left in a hurry, appreciating having eight cylinders firing at once.

But, back to the border crossings. As mentioned above, it is rare that the officials directly solicit bribes. Rather, they set up a massive difficulty and let the traveler suggest that some payments might facilitate the process. I must admit that my stubbornness and my intense displeasure in being forced into these situations generally results in my not paying the fees. Rather, I almost always, in as friendly but as clearly determined a way as I can, continue to discuss my perception that the additional fees may not be appropriate in this particular case. What I have to do is invest much time, patience, and humility to show, in an apparently friendly way, that I do not intend to pay the extra fee, and am willing to spend quite a while to achieve that end. I usually succeed, but I end up spending a great deal of time in border crossings. It often takes us three or four hours, or more, to cross a frontier.

In getting hit with a fee, the important thing to distinguish is its officialness. Some fees, such as for fumigating the vehicle, are legitimate and official, and they give you a receipt for the service (to contaminate all food inside the vehicle with a powerful herbicide-insecticide, and cause a chemical stench that lasts for hours). Others are less official, and you certainly do not get and do not ask for a receipt, but they are relatively routine and must be paid without protest. One must be aware of sudden inflations of the fees, and those can be negotiated. It is along the next area of the spectrum that I object: the ad hoc fees that get added when the opportunity is perceived. So, I usually fight for principle and often I win. I will never calculate the dollars per hour figure, but we are usually able to do both sides of a border within three or four hours and for $50 or so.

When we were going to Quirigua, we reached the Guatemalan border and began dealing with the Salvadorans in order to exit the country. We went through the myriad hassles and were ready to enter Guatemala— or rather start the myriad hassles to try to enter Guatemala—after a couple hours. During the early part of the process, something that one of our group said irritated a Guatemalan customs official, and he started putting up additional hassles. It got worse and looked virtually impossible for us to get into Guatemala, when my wife and I decided to try our most bold (i.e., desperate) move. One of our problems really was our fault, as we had forgotten to get a Guatemalan visa stamped into Kayla's passport. Kayla was only one year old at the time, and we realized we had forgotten to get her visa when we got the others the previous week at the Guatemalan embassy. As we perceived our mistake, he relished it, as he had us by the "huevos,"[8] as they say. However, we were very determined to get to Quirigua by nightfall, as we knew the kind of party the Quirigua crew had waiting for us. So we pulled out the heavy ammunition. As my wife, Fran, calmly walked out to the car and retrieved a large, clear plastic bag with Kayla's dirty diapers inside it, along with a short stack of clean diapers, I began to calmly admit to the official that yes, he was correct, the error was ours, and we were very sorry. What took him aback was my calm following sentence, that, in concordance with their laws, Kayla would not be able to accompany us, and she would have to stay with him and the other officials ("swarthy band of brigands," I thought to myself) at the frontier. Now, they would have to change her diaper thus, they would have to feed her thus, they would have to entertain her thus, so she did not start crying and fussing, and so on. As Fran came up to the counter with the dirty and clean diapers, she informed them that they would need to wash and dry the dirty diapers soon, as the clean ones would last only a few more hours. We were surprised and pleased that he took us seriously, and he began rapidly scurrying for an alternative solution. Under no circumstances would we actually have left our daughter there alone, even for a second, but he did not know that. Amazing. He came up with the alternative plan surprisingly fast, suggesting that Kayla could go with us, along with her dirty and clean diapers, but her passport would be left with him at the border office. Thus, in a bizarre way, the problem of the passport not having a visa was resolved by the passport staying at the frontier, even though Kayla would be entering the country with neither passport nor visa. We thanked him profusely, suppressed profanations, and headed into Guatemala toward Quirigua.

We barely had breathed a sigh of relief when we came around a bend and were stopped by a military roadblock. We later found out that a prominent businessman had just been kidnapped in Guatemala City, and roadblocks were being set up throughout the country to try to find him and his captors. First they checked under our luggage in the back to see if there was someone hidden underneath, and poor Chris had the scare of his life when a guard opened the back door of the van and got the muzzle of the M-16 assault rifle inadvertently jammed up his nostril. Things did not get much lighter when they lined us up, counted noses, counted passports, and matched passport photos with individual people. There were seven of us: me, Fran, Kayla, and four University of Colorado students. There were six passports. Now we really thought we were in trouble. But much to our surprise, they ended their inspection by telling us that all was in order and that we could proceed. We lost little time in getting out of there, but we speculated for a long time about what had happened. Did they count Kayla? Did they think that she was too young to have a passport or need one? Did they think that she was somehow covered by mine or Fran's?

Somewhat the worse for wear, we finally did roll into the Quirigua project camp late in the evening. After getting hotel rooms for less than a dollar each (and yes, you do get what you pay for), and a memorable party, most of us hit the sack at the hotel shortly after midnight. Chris and Kevin continued the revelry for another two hours but found the front door of the hotel locked when they got there. Being thoughtful and considerate, they decided that they would cause less inconvenience by going around back, climbing over the back wall, and sneaking into the hotel rather than knocking and awaking the manager. That might have worked had they not missed by one property. Unfortunately, they hopped the wrong wall and fell over on top of a large, sleeping pig that awoke with such squawks and hootings that every dog in a three-block radius awoke and began barking. What a commotion. That awoke all people within a four-block radius. And not only that, the maid refused to wash their clothes the next day, they were so smelly and filthy. Such is life in the tropics.

CONCLUSIONS

We consider ourselves fortunate to have the opportunity to conduct research in El Salvador, particularly at the Ceren site. The site provides us with an unprecedented opportunity to understand what family life was like 1400 years ago, even to the point of knowing just what was growing in their gardens and milpas, where the mice were in their thatch roofs, and which polychrome pots were for food serving. Because all artifacts are there where the Ceren residents left them, we have the opportunity of answering questions that nobody had even thought to ask before. For instance, we are learning how they looked after their sharp knives: they put them up in the thatch near the doorway of structures. We know quite a lot about what they grew and ate. Their staple was corn, aided by beans, squash, chiles, tomatoes, manioc, achiote, cacao, and various nuts and fruits from nearby trees.

Before excavating at the Ceren site, we had no idea of the sophistication and variation in their domestic architecture. We did not know about their bajareque walls, corner columns, lattice windows, strong roofs, lintels, cornices, and the like. We had no idea that they were also making solid adobe "rammed-earth" walls and earthen domes.

It will take many more seasons of excavations to more fully understand the site in its environment, but great strides have been taken during the past few years. Much of that accomplishment has been because of the dedication of Salvadoran workers, graduate students from the University of Colorado, and an international team of volcanologists, geophysicists, and biologists. Fortunately, that research is conducted within a strong conservation ethic, to give the site the longest future possible.

On the personal side, we consider ourselves fortunate to have been accepted into the lives of many Salvadoran families. Some of the best friends we have live in humble homes in the Salvadoran countryside, and we wish them the best of good fortune in an uncertain future. The Ceren site has enriched all of our lives.

Endnotes

1. These mean precipitation figures illustrate what I call the "fallacy of the mean." That an average of 1700 millimeters of rain falls in the area might lead one to conclude that there is abundant moisture for agriculture, but that is not always true. For some reason, in our culture we pay too much attention to the mean figures and often call them "normal." Thus, we worry about a year that is "below normal" in precipitation, or a child that is "below normal" in classroom achievement.

2. No, this is not an inadvertent example of gender discrimination. I deliberately use the masculine form because males are the agriculturalists in Central America, in the past and in the present. In fact, many ethnic groups build roles into tradition and religion. The Maya view human life as a close analog to the plant growth cycle, believing that the maturing crops represent the future sustenance of society. Thus, it is the male who plants the seed, both in the agricultural and the reproductive senses. The seed is received and nurtured by mother earth, or the mother of the child. Then, the young plant sprouts and grows to maturation when it produces its own next generation, and then it fades and dies back into the earth from whence it came. Death follows birth, which follows death, in cycle after cycle. In fact, they take this one step farther and believe that life comes from death, and vice versa, and death is necessary for life. Thus they unite into a single dynamic concept what we often think of as opposites or mutually exclusive conditions.

3. Local inhabitants claim that the Salvadoran air force was instructed to bomb the crater, to re-initiate the eruptions. There are some doubts about that, however, because the crater is only a kilometer across. Local residents claim that the Salvadoran air force could never hit a target that small (!).

4. The use of a proctoscope has generated a few facetious comments. Probably the best is the title of a paper purportedly to be presented at some future archaeological professional meetings: "Viewing the Site as a Whole: Proctological Perspectives on Prehistory." In contrast to most professional papers, all potential authors are scurrying for last place in the series of authors.

5. So how can one take the temperature of something that fell hot 1400 years ago, but cooled within hours or days afterward? Richard Hoblitt (1983) used an ingenious technique called progressive thermal demagnetization. The technique is based on the fact that all magma chunks have millions of microscopic iron particles. When the magma is very hot, all of the particles are free to move and act like miniature compasses. They point toward the north magnetic pole. When the chunk of magma cools, the particles become "frozen" in place and continue pointing toward the north magnetic pole. The hotter the magma, the more the particles line up. A magma that was more cool when it landed will have a lower percentage of particles lining up. Thus, the degree of magnetic alignment is proportional to the temperature. The magma clasts

from the Laguna Caldera eruption, by this analysis, were above the highest temperature that the technique can measure, 575 degrees Celsius.

6. One time when Kevin Black was leading a survey party, he was stopped by the armed guard of a large plot of land, who rode up on horseback and asked if he had permission. Kevin said no, but that he would like to get it. The guard said it would have to be written, but it was not clear where Kevin should get it. After considerable discussion, Kevin offered to write the letter of permission and sign it, essentially giving himself permission to walk the land, and that was accepted. The guard was told that all permissions must be written, and he had fulfilled his obligation!

7. A group of people doing an assessment of the earthquake and the relief effort noted that all age groups were equally killed by the falling adobe bricks from collapsing walls, with the exception of infants. At first they did not understand why infants survived better than other age groups. But when it was pointed out that infants traditionally sleep in between the mother and father, in part so they can nurse during the night, it became clear. Many deaths could have been prevented had people continued using the seismic-resistant bajareque architecture such as that at the Ceren site.

8. Translated literally: "eggs."

References

Adams, R. N.
1981 "The Dynamics of Societal Diversity: Notes from Nicaragua for a Sociology of Survival." *American Ethnologist* 8: 1-20.

Arnould, E.
1986 "Households." In A. and J. Kuper, eds. *The Social Science Encyclopedia*, 364–366. London: Routledge and Kegan Paul.

Barron Castro, R.
1942 *La Poblacion de El Salvador*. Madrid: Inst. G. Fernandez de Oviedo.

Beaudry, Marilyn
1983 "The Ceramics of the Zapotitan Valley." In Sheets, ed. 1983: 161–190.

Beaudry, Marilyn, and David Tucker
1989 "Household 1 Area Excavations." In Sheets & McKee, eds. 1989: 29–40.

Black, Kevin
1983 The Zapotitan Valley Archeological Survey. In Sheets, ed. *Archeology and Volcanism in Central America: The Zapotitan Valley of El Salvador*. University of Texas Press, Austin. pp. 62–97.

Blake, M.
1987 "Paso de la Amada: An Early Formative Chiefdom in Chiapas, Mexico." Paper presented at the 86th Annual Meeting, American Anthropological Association, Chicago.

Chang, K., ed.
1968 *Settlement Archaeology*. Palo Alto: National Press.

Daugherty, Howard E.
1969 *Man-induced Ecologic Change in El Salvador*. Ph.D. Dissertation, Geography, University of California, Los Angeles. Ann Arbor: University Microfilms.

Dean, C. G.
1987 "Northern Honduran Subsistence Kitchens and their Contents." Paper presented at the Society for American Archaeology Meetings, Toronto.

Eaton, J.
1975 *Ancient Agricultural Farmsteads in the Rio Bec Region of Yucatan*. Contributions of the University of California Archaeological Research Facility, Berkeley. No. 27, pp. 56–82.

Flannery, K. V., ed.
1976 *The Early Mesoamerican Village*. New York: Academic.

Flannery, K. V., and M. C. Winter
1976 Analyzing Household Activities. *The Early Mesoamerican Village*, K. Flannery, ed. pp. 34–47.

Gerstle, Andrea I.
    1989 Excavations at Structure 3, Ceren, 1989. P. Sheets and B. McKee, eds. pp. 59–80.

Gerstle, Andrea I.
    1990 "1990 Operation 4 Preliminary Report." P. Sheets and B. McKee, eds. 1990
        Preliminary Report, Ceren. Anthropology, University of Colorado, Boulder.

Hammond, N., D. Pring, R. Wilk, S. Donaghey, F. Saul, E. Wing, A. Miller, and L.
Feldman
    1979 "The Earliest Lowland Maya: Definition of the Swasey Phase." *American
        Antiquity* 44:92–110.

Hoblitt, R. P.
    1983 Volcanic Events at the Ceren Site. In *Archeology and Volcanism in Central
        America: The Zapotitan Valley of El Salvador.* P.D. Sheets, ed. Austin: University
        of Texas Press. pp. 144–146.

Kramer, C.
    1982 *Village Ethnoarchaeology: Rural Iran in Archaeological Perspective.* New York:
        Academic Press.

Lange, F., and C. R. Rydberg
    1972 "Abandonment and Post-abandonment Behavior at a Costa Rican House-site."
        American Antiquity 37: 419–432.

Laslett, P.
    1972 Introduction: The History of the Family. In P. Laslett and R. Wall eds. *Household
        and Family in Past Time.* pp. 1–89. Cambridge: Cambridge University Press.

Loker, W. M.
    1983 Recent Geophysical Explorations at Ceren. In *Archeology and Volcanism in
        Central America: The Zapotitan Valley of El Salvador.* P.D. Sheets, ed. Austin:
        University of Texas Press. pp. 254–274.

McBryde, Felix Webster
    1947 *Cultural and Historical Geography of Southwest Guatemala.* Smithsonian
        Institution, Institute of Social Anthropology, Publication #4. Washington D. C.

McKee, Brian R.
    1989 Excavations at Structure Complex 2. Sheets, P. and B. McKee, eds. pp. 41–58.

McKee, Brian R.
    1990a Structure 7 Excavations. Sheets, P. and B. McKee, eds. 1990.

McKee, Brian R.
    1990b 1990–1991 Structure 9 Excavations. P. Sheets and B. McKee, eds. 1990
        Preliminary Report, Ceren. Anthropology, University of Colorado, Boulder.

Miller, C. Dan
    1989 Stratigraphy of Volcanic Deposits at El Ceren. In *1989 Archaeological
        Investigations at the Ceren Site, El Salvador: A Preliminary Report,* P. Sheets and B.
        McKee, eds. Manuscript, Anthropology, University of Colorado, Boulder.
        pp. 8–19.

Murphy, Sean
    1989 Casting Organic Materials. Sheets and McKee, eds. 1989: 27–28.

Netting, R., R. Wilk, and E. Arnould, eds.
    1984 *Households: Domestic and Historical Studies of the Domestic Group.* Berkeley:
        University of California Press.

Olson, Gerald W.
  1983 An Evaluation of Soil Properties and Potentials in Different Volcanic
     Deposits. Sheets, ed. 1983: 52–61.

Parry, W.
  1987 *Chipped Stone Tools in Formative Oaxaca, Mexico: Their Procurement, Production
     and Use*. Memoirs, University of Michigan, Museum of Anthropology, 20.

Reyna de Aguilar, Maria Luisa
  1991 "Und Verdadera Joya...Joya de Ceren; Flora Autoctona Salvadoreña." *Pankia*
     10:2: 3–9. (Jardin Botanico, San Salvador, El Salvador).

Rice, Prudence M.
  1989 *Pottery Analysis: A Sourcebook*. Chicago: University of Chicago Press.

Ringle, W., and E. Andrews V
  1983 "Formative Residences at Komchen, Yucatan, Mexico." Paper presented at
     the Society for American Archaeology Annual Meeting.

Sheets, Payson, and Fran Mandel Sheets
  1990 Excavations of Structure 12, Ceren, 1990–1991. In P. Sheets and B. McKee,
     eds. 1990 Preliminary Report, Ceren. Anthropology, University of
     Colorado, Boulder.

Sheets, Payson D., ed.
  1983 *Archeology and Volcanism in Central America: The Zapotitan Valley of El
     Salvador*. Austin: University of Texas Press.

Sheets, Payson D., and Brian R. McKee, eds.
  1989 *1989 Archaeological Investigations at the Ceren Site, El Salvador: A Preliminary
     Report*. Manuscript, Department of Anthropology, University of Colorado,
     Boulder.

Sheets, Payson D., and Brian R. McKee, eds.
  1990 *1990 Research at the Ceren Site, El Salvador: A Preliminary Report*. Manuscript,
     Department of Anthropology, University of Colorado, Boulder.

Sheets, Payson D., Harriet F. Beaubien, Marilyn Beaudry, Andrea Gerstle, Brian
McKee, C. Dan Miller, Hartmut Spetzler, and David B. Tucker
  1990 "Household Archaeology at Ceren, El Salvador." *Ancient Mesoamerica*
     1:81–90. Cambridge University Press.

Southward, Judith A., and Diana C. Kamilli
  1983 Preliminary Study of Selected Ceramics from the Ceren House. Sheets, ed.
     1983, pp. 147–151.

Spencer, C.
  1981 "Spatial Organization of an Early Formative Household." In M. Whalen
     Excavations at Santo Domingo Tomaltepec, pp. 195–203. University of
     Michigan, Museum of Anthropology, Memoirs 12.

Spetzler, Hartmut, and David Tucker
  1989 Geophysical Research at Ceren. In *1989 Archaeological Investigations at the
     Ceren Site, El Salvador: A Preliminary Report*, P. Sheets and B. McKee, eds.
     pp. 20–21. Manuscript, Anthropology, University of Colorado, Boulder.

Stone, Doris
  1948 "The Northern Highland Tribes: The Lenca." In *Handbook of South American
     Indians*, J. Steward, ed. Volume 4, pp. 205–218.

Wauchope, R.
   1938 *Modern Maya Houses: A Study of Their Archaeological Significance.*
       Washington: Carnegie Institution of Washington, Publication 502.

Webster, D., and N. Gonlin
   1988 "Household Remains of the Humblest Maya." *Journal of Field Archaeology* 15:
       169–189.

Whalen, M.
   1981 *Excavations at Santo Domingo Tomaltepec: Evolution of a Formative Community
       in the Valley of Oaxaca, Mexico.* University of Michigan, Museum of
       Anthropology, Memoirs 12.

Wilk, R.
   1988 "Maya Household Organization: Evidence and Analogies." In *Household and
       Community in the Mesoamerican Past,* Wilk and Ashmore, eds. Albuquerque:
       University of New Mexico Press, pp. 135–151.

Wilk, R., and W. Ashmore, eds.
   1988 *Household and Community in the Mesoamerican Past.* Albuquerque: University
       of New Mexico Press.

Wilk, R., and W. Rathje
   1982 "Household Archaeology." *American Behavioral Scientist* 25: 617–639.

Willey, G. R., W. Bullard, Jr., J. Glass, and J. Gifford
   1965 *Prehistoric Maya Settlements in the Belize Valley.* Papers, Peabody Museum,
       Harvard University. Vol. 54.

Wilshusen, R. H.
   1986 "The Relationship between Abandonment Mode and Ritual Use in Pueblo I
       Anasazi Protokivas." *Journal of Field Archaeology* 13: 245–54.

Winter, M. C.
   1976 The Archeological Household Cluster in the Valley of Oaxaca. In *The Early
       Mesoamerican Village,* K. Flannery, ed. NY: Academic Press, pp. 25–31.

Wisdom, C.
   1940 *The Chorti Indians of Guatemala.* Chicago: University of Chicago Press.

Zier, Christian J.
   1983 The Ceren Site: A Classic Period Maya Residence and Agricultural Field in
       the Zapotitan Valley. Sheets, ed. 1983: 119–143.

Index

147